SO YOU WANT TO BE A COP

SO YOU WANT TO BE A COP

What Everyone Should Know Before Entering a Law Enforcement Career

Alley Evola

ROWMAN & LITTLEFIELD
Lanham • Boulder • New York • London

Published by Rowman & Littlefield
A wholly owned subsidary of The Rowman & Littlefield Publishing Group, Inc.
4501 Forbes Boulevard, Suite 200, Lanham, Maryland 20706
www.rowman.com

Unit A, Whitacre Mews, 26-34 Stannary Street, London SE11 4AB

British Library Cataloguing in Publication Information Available

Library of Congress Cataloging-in-Publication Data Available

ISBN 978-1-5381-0147-6 (cloth : alk. paper)
ISBN 978-1-5381-0148-3 (electronic)

∞ ™ The paper used in this publication meets the minimum requirements of
American National Standard for Information Sciences Permanence of Paper for
Printed Library Materials, ANSI/NISO Z39.48-1992.

Printed in the United States of America

*For my parents, Phyllis and Jim Evola, whose uncondi-
tional love and selfless devotion ensured that I would
have every opportunity to succeed.*

*For Jacki, whose unfailing support and love has always
been there for me through good times and bad. There's
no one I'd rather share this journey with than you.*

*For Drs. Ed Kimbrell, Robert Petersen, Glenn Hime-
baugh, and Alan Hibbard, who encouraged me to find my
voice and use it inside and outside the conventions of
academia.*

CONTENTS

INTRODUCTION

There is a plethora of books out there by police officers for the general public sharing war stories that titillate, pump adrenaline, and entertain. This is not one of those books. While I hope you are entertained, I would prefer that you come away from reading this book better informed and perhaps a bit more sympathetic to the lifestyle the law enforcement officer in the United States is obliged to live in order to protect you, your loved ones, and your property.

However, this book is mostly for those of you who dream of being a cop. If you are considering a career in law enforcement in the United States, there are a few things you need to know up front. These are things that many law enforcement officers will not tell you and things that you probably won't believe, even after I share them. I'm relating this information to help you make a more informed decision about a career choice that will impact your future and the future of your family.

Sharing my personal experiences as a veteran law enforcement officer will give you an insider's view into the world of law enforcement in this country in the twenty-first century.

This information is not intended to be advice, to serve as a how-to manual, or to in any way take the place of professional law enforcement training. This is just my personal opinion and experience and should be taken as such.

The names and locations relating to actual events that I address in this book have been changed to protect the privacy of those involved. That being said, the circumstances surrounding those incidents and the investigations that often followed are based on real-life acts, both experienced firsthand and observed.

I

MYTH VERSUS FACT

From Dreaming to Testing and Entering the Force

Three ear-splitting tones rip through the night air from your patrol car radio. Your adrenaline spikes, your heartbeat doubles, you flip emergency equipment on, and you punch the accelerator to the floor. As you zigzag in and out of traffic, cross over into the oncoming lane, and cuss the geezer who is at a complete stop in his vintage Plymouth in the middle of the road while trying to figure out where all that noise is coming from, you call out your position to dispatch.

Instantaneously, you're in the middle of a breakneck-speed convoy of blinding blue strobe lights and deafening noise. The bad guy you are all chasing is packing a handgun and is high on crank, adrenaline, and arrogance. He has just split open a grandma's head to snatch her Social Security check money she just cashed. He doesn't care that he's running red lights. That he's endangering other motorists. That he could cause a wreck and kill himself and the cops on his bumper. He's hell-bent on getting away no matter what the cost.

Suddenly, a crash and a cloud of dirt and debris punches the air twenty feet above the roadway like an improvised explosive device (IED) going off. The red taillights of the patrol cars ahead of you light up in unison. You and the other officers slam your cars into park, un-holster your forty-caliber handguns, hit the ground running, and sprint toward the flaming getaway car that is upside down against a bent and splintered telephone pole.

Then you fight through the flames, ignore the fact that the car could explode in your face, and drag the bad guy to safety. You even call an ambulance for him. Then you spend the next six hours trying to come off the adrenaline rush and filling out paperwork.

And you spend the next three days talking to anyone who will listen about it, dream about it over and over, and can't wait until it happens again.

Sound like fun? Then you've been watching too much television or you must want to be a police officer, or both.

Well, wonderful, but I think there are a few things you might want to wrap your head around before you sprint headlong into this life full of adventure.

First, the career trajectory of a police officer is more akin to a marathon, not a forty-yard dash, and figuratively speaking, it's a hard slog, because the runners are heavily weighted down with the burdens of posttraumatic stress disorder (PTSD), heart disease, diabetes, insomnia, divorce, infighting, backbiting, anger-management issues, domestic abuse, alcohol and drug abuse, politics, corruption, prejudices, vices, debt, eating disorders, nightmares, guilt, guile, envy, sloth, lawsuits, and so much more. The runners are, of course, police officers; those already out of the race and those who are on their last legs and may not even know it. All this from those adrenaline-spiking experiences like high-speed chases, gun fights, and life behind the badge you so crave.

According to Rich Dittmar, "The average police officer dies within five years after retirement and reportedly has a life expectancy of twelve years less than that of other people.[1]

Why?

The so-called *life* of a police officer does not even remotely resemble the sensationalized-for-entertainment reality seen daily on television and in the movies. It is, however, a way of life. The kicker is that it's not a healthy, joyous way of life. The entertainment industry depicts virtuous, dedicated, overworked, anguish-riddled law enforcement officers who put it all on the line for the people they serve, but who are, in the end, rewarded ten-fold because they know they have fought the good fight and have done the noble deed. They sacrificed their comfort and happiness for the better good. Their families suffer along with them in their own way, but are also rewarded by having the love and devotion of a real-life, action-figure hero with whom they always feel safe and secure.

Pure fiction.

Here's fact: I was a self-important, proud, and arrogant rookie cop raring to be cut loose on my own to right the wrongs of society. I say "cut loose" because my department, and many other departments throughout the United States, operates single-officer patrol units. Until rookies complete field training and then the mentoring program, they ride with a senior officer on their shifts.

The mentoring program follows field training, after which most new officers in the United States are allowed to work on their own. The purpose of the mentoring program, according to our department's administration, is to provide a new officer with an opportunity to continue to learn the layout of the city and the real-world job under the tutelage of an experienced officer. The senior officer functions as a mentor and a safety net for the new officer. Ostensibly, the purpose of the program is for *public consumption*. However, the ulterior motives of the department higher-ups, and they always have them, are to insulate the city against liability resulting from your rookie mistake, and to create a budgetary cushion of six months between the time you complete your initial training and the time the city has to buy a new police car for you.

So what does the mentoring program really boil down to? Risk management and fiscal controls. Get used to it; these are two of the strongest driving forces that direct how a police department operates. No, not citizen safety, not officer safety, not crime prevention, and not even to make the world a better place. Money, power, and politics drive police departments as surely as they drive corporations.

Being a successful cog in your police department's wheelhouse can at times be a source of stress you will have to deal with, as well as the mental and emotional stress of the job that you will need to deal with on the home front. So what do you think now? Think you'll be different? Think that you'll beat the odds? That you will be immune from those problems? Think that since you know about the evils, that you will ensure that you aren't poisoned by the profession? Well, I hope you're right. I wasn't so lucky, but others have had different outcomes with their careers.

The good news is that you can't just stumble into becoming a law enforcement officer. You have to work really, really hard at it. The process is long and difficult for good reason. Beyond the initial six months of academic testing, interviewing, the thorough background check, and the polygraph, physical, and psychological testing lies a long year of training including the police academy and the field training program.

This foundation theoretically ensures that cops are stable, unemotional, well-prepared, and ready and able to interject themselves into crisis situations and bring them to a successful conclusion. You must be ready to take effective control and to protect the citizens and their property from whatever threat arises. You must respond without hesitation and professionally to a wide range of threats including natural disasters, motor vehicle accidents, speeding motorists, impaired drivers, road rage, thieves, bank robbers, domestic disturbances, lost children, hostage situations, gang activities, mass murder, school violence, and the occasional cow in the road that needs to be herded back into its pasture. Of course, this is not a comprehensive list, but you get the idea.

When I applied to become a police officer, it seemed so simple, so innocuous. I mailed a three-inch by five-inch postcard to the city's human resources department indicating my desire to test for an open police-officer position. Then I waited, and waited, then waited some more. At last, I received a call from a human resources specialist extending a verbal invitation, to be followed by a written invitation, to appear at a local library at the given date and time so the police department could determine if I was smart enough and physically fit enough to do the job. See, nothing is simple. Getting a career in law enforcement can be a difficult and complicated process.

The civil service exam I sat for drew what looked like a cattle call from central casting for a made-for-television rookie cop show—macho guys, sturdy and capable chicks, no-nonsense veterans, urban gunslingers, adrenaline junkies, idealistic do-gooders, little men with little-man complexes, and garden-variety nut jobs.

On the day of the exam, I arrived early and waited in line outside of the library talking with the other wannabes. At the precise time indicated on the invitation, more than three hundred of us were admitted to a large meeting room, provided with two number-two pencils, and a one hundred-question test booklet. Upon completion of our written exam, each candidate's booklet was scored. If you scored in the seventieth percentile or above, you went outside and stood in line again to complete the physical agility course.

The physical agility course was easier than I had expected. I would later learn that the course was designed so every sworn officer, especially the old-timers with the beer barrel belly hanging over their duty belt, could successfully complete it during their annual in-service training. I had rigorously trained for the course for weeks, so I was barely winded when I passed it. But keep in mind that this was my experience, and the course you encounter may be tougher depending on the department and the standards they adhere to. Next they gave me a date for my interview before the chief's review board.

A few days later, I entered a closed-door room and sat at the end of a large conference table surrounded by police supervisors in uniform and police administrators: the chief of police and several commanders, lieutenants, and sergeants. A friend of my father's was a sergeant on the force, so I already had a good idea of the questions that might be asked.

Before you get the wrong impression here, let me explain. Many police officers are hired as a direct result of their relationships with officers already on the department. Nepotism is the rule, not the exception in law enforcement. It's better to take a chance on the known than on the unknown. Or, to say it another way, it helps to know someone.

Among the many "intellectually challenging" questions posed to me by the brain-trust of the department were:

What were the last three books you read?

Why do you want to be a police officer?

Where do you see yourself in five years?

Sound familiar? Typical old-school, hackneyed job-interview questions. But what might surprise you are the answers the department prefers to hear. For example, when responding to why you want to become a police officer, they do not want to hear you say, "I want to protect and serve." Nor do they want to hear, "Because my daddy was a police officer."

An ideal response might be, "I think I'd be great at this job because," or "I'm really interested in the work." The last person they want to hire is someone who has watched too many episodes of *COPS* and just wants in on the action. If you think you are going to be a superhero, you might want to audition for your local community theater and save yourself some time and embarrassment.

Oh, did that sound sarcastic? Sarcasm: it's the second language of the police officer. We'll get to that a little later.

After completing the testing and interview process, you go home and wait some more, likely several weeks. Then one day your phone will ring.

The human resources generalist tells you that the chief of police is offering you "a conditional employment opportunity." It's your first taste of law enforcement. Your adrenaline spikes, your heartbeat doubles, and you can hardly keep yourself from belting out a rebel yell. It's your first taste of the unpredictable but addictive blast of adrenaline.

But hold your water. The "conditional" part of the offer is based upon your successful completion of the polygraph examination, psychological examination, and physical examination. Barring any problems there, about three months later you should be ready to report for your first day, which will probably consist of filing paperwork in the records division of the police department, but your first day nonetheless. Welcome to law enforcement.

2

YOU'RE HIRED! NOW WHAT?

Every law enforcement agency is different, but where I started the first week of my life as a police officer began with the initial rite of passage: Limbo Week. Actually, my first four months at the police department could have been called "Invisible Week," because I didn't exist as far as the officer corps was concerned. Frankly, becoming invisible, or flying under the radar, as many police officers refer to it, is an important skill to develop in your law enforcement career, so use this time wisely. Learn from it. In fact, learn from everything. Be a big blue sponge.

My greeting this week by our training sergeant went something like this: "Eeeeevvvoooahheehhhlaaa? How do you say that? Oh, Evola (Eee-vo-lah). Okay, Evola, this is Limbo Week, and we'll be getting your paperwork in order, issuing you gear, getting you qualified on your handgun, and getting you sworn in. In the meantime, keep your mouth shut, your eyes and ears open, and report to Ms. Smith in records. She'll tell you what to do. Oh, one more thing. Keep your mouth shut!"

During Limbo Week, when I wasn't filing records or filling out paperwork in the administrative offices of the police department, I observed police officers as they came and went from the station. Apparently I was invisible, because during this time, I was not talked to, but rather, I was talked around.

You have to be with the department for a while before you become part of the family, and even when you earn a place at the table, you'll come to realize that membership isn't as great as you hoped it would be in the brotherhood of law enforcement officers. You know, "The Thin Blue Line."

While it's true to the general perception that a police department is a family, more accurately it's a dysfunctional family. The company line is all about professionalism and unity, but inside the hallowed halls of the station, officers are tearing each other up overtly and covertly. Big egos, bigger ambitions, and politics create a figuratively cut-throat environment. Occasionally, we'll patch up the verbal injury we've visited on each other, but generally speaking, it's not a build-you-up kind of place. If you want someone who loves you unconditionally and attends lovingly to your slightest boo-boos, go home to your mother. And remember what the famous blues musician from Mississippi, B.B. King, said, "Only your mamma loves you, and she could be jivin' too!"

Nonetheless, I'd be lying if I told you I wasn't thrilled to be on the inside of the mysterious and exciting blue curtain. Outwardly, I appeared to be invisible and quiet, but inside, I was jumping around, yelling, and high-fiving myself. I was a police officer, the city employee badge with my officer title hanging from the lanyard around my neck proved that, right? Boy, was I naïve! I hadn't even been sworn in yet.

As Limbo Week progressed, I was ferried to the police supply and uniform store where I was fitted for my standard issue of three uniforms, the training sergeant selected my duty gear, and I was even allowed to choose which type of clip board I would like to hold the citations and fine sheets I would issue someday. I was in police heaven.

Wait. Three uniforms? We worked a four-day, ten-hour-per-day schedule. No, the math doesn't work, and thus, the first rule of becoming a law enforcement officer: expect the unexpected. You have to adapt. Constantly. Forever. Not bitch or whine—adapt.

Change is one of the few constants in law enforcement, so be prepared for it. Expect it. Embrace it. Roll with it. My first sergeant summed it up well: "Alley, if there's something you don't like here, wait two weeks and it will change." He was right.

Near the end of the week, I, along with another rookie, was issued my duty weapon, which at my agency was the Sig Sauer Sig Pro 2340. Our training sergeant, who was a firearms instructor, took us to the county sheriff department's range to qualify on our weapons for the first time. I shot a respectable score in the eightieth percentile on the qualification course with my handgun, and I scored in the ninetieth percentile with the department-issued shotgun. Not bad for a rookie who had never fired a handgun in her life. At the time, an officer needed a minimum score of 72 percent to qualify with a hand gun. Since that time, the score required has increased to 78 percent.

Now, fully armed with an arsenal and tedious paperwork-processing expertise, Limbo Week Friday came, and it was time to be sworn in. There were only two of us selected to be sworn in from more than three hundred applicants who applied for the position of police officer with the department. We were both women. You have to think in terms of that federal guideline here that requires 10 percent of the department's sworn personnel to be female. I waited nervously in the police department training room for the chief of police, his secretary, and a few people they rounded up from the administrative pool to make the ceremony look important. I was excited to take the next step in finally becoming a representative of the law, or in my television-affected mind, "The Law."

Taking the Oath of Office was a defining moment. In my mind, that made it official. Of course, I had a lot to learn, as I was still within my probationary year.

The chief asked us to raise our right hand and to repeat after him, "I, (state your name), do solemnly swear that as a member of the police department, I will support the Constitution of the State of (fill in the blank) and the Constitution of the United States of America, and that I will perform with fidelity and faithfully execute the duties of this office to the best of my ability, so help me God." And with that solemn promise before God, the chief of police, a secretary, and a handful of other administrative strangers, on June 21, 2002, I officially became a police officer.

In my innocent self-satisfaction with the ceremony and all it took for me to get to this point, I had no idea what I had done to my future, but I was damn proud of it.

On week two, I was assigned to my primary field training officer (FTO). This was the guy who would teach me the ropes and evaluate my progress. Later on in my career, I would be promoted to FTO and play that important role in the development of new police officers. All FTOs have their own style and way of doing things. Even though they are supposed to subscribe to a standard of evaluation that is used by every FTO and across the pool of trainees, they don't. The reality is that every FTO allows personal and professional prejudices to color his or her evaluation of a trainee. I was no exception.

After swearing in, it was off to Scenario Training. During Scenario Training, I was supervised by several FTOs. Scenario Training was new to my department and in reality, an experiment. Today, however, this type of training is prevalent across the United States, and as a new recruit, you can probably expect to encounter it in one form or another. My fellow recruits and I were the guinea pigs. In the past, new recruits assigned to an FTO began the first phase of field training, riding shotgun with the FTO. They would carry with them what was affectionately referred to as a "Rook Book" that contained general orders (departmental policies), street maps, and annotated code books detailing state traffic and criminal laws. They would refer to these reference materials when they hit a snag and, if necessary, they could also seek advice from their FTO.

But now, Scenario Training consisted of meeting at the police-department training room each morning with our FTOs, a classroom session on a topic of departmental policy and procedure or state law, and then a trip to the Fraternal Order of Police Lodge (FOP). There trainees sit in their patrol cars in the gravel parking lot and take simulated calls over the radio from our FTOs located in the lodge, who created scenarios and then played the roles of suspect and/or victim. Once they decided on the scenario and who would play what role, they dispatched the call to us over the radio on an auxiliary channel, and we theoretically responded from our cars, sitting stationary in the parking lot.

One of my training scenarios was a domestic disturbance call. While my back-up officer, a fellow recruit, spoke with the female role-player located just outside of the house but within my peripheral vision, I spoke with the male subject inside the house. He was seated at a desk. It seemed in my unindoctrinated mind like a routine call, so what was the point of the scenario? The hammer lying beside his left hand that I failed to notice was the point. Before the scenario was over, I had been beaten to death by that hammer. It was a sobering exercise and one that no doubt saved my life on more than a couple of occasions during my career. Officer safety for me and my fellow officers was, from that point forward, always on my mind. Lesson learned: be acutely aware of your surroundings. Your observation could make the difference between living and dying, between going home at the end of your shift and going to the morgue.

The new seven-week Scenario Training was a success and was continued in our department until 2010, when the department decided to return to the old way of doing things. What a shame, because the short amount of time invested and the minute dedication of resources paid off. The lives of officers were saved. Scenario Training is indispensable in new police officer development.

An aspiring police officer needs to understand that donning the uniform and getting behind the wheel of a patrol car doesn't make you a law enforcement officer. Sure, you'll never forget your first time you drive a patrol car—I sure didn't—but I still wasn't a cop and somewhere, deep down inside, I knew it. So did my instructors.

While we are on the subject of molding new law enforcement officers, let me offer you another job tip to keep in mind. "Police officer" is a job title. It doesn't define who you are and it shouldn't, ever! When it starts doing that, you need to find a new occupation. It's one of many points of light I shined on my trainees as an FTO. I only wish someone had shared that tip with me early in my career, or if someone did, that I had listened.

Yet another aspect of every new officer's training is attending the police academy. Not everyone who signs on with a police department goes straight to the police academy. Some might go when they hire-on, and others might attend six months later, or still others may attend at the end of their first year with the force.

Just as when a recruit attends the police academy varies across agencies and jurisdictions, so do the phases of training. A new officer might ride with an FTO, who does the majority of the work, instructing the rookie in any and all situations they encounter. Other FTOs may lay back and let their trainee give it his or her best shot and then educate the trainee accordingly afterward. But more importantly, the FTO will evaluate the new officer's performance to aid the training sergeant to determine if the recruit progresses to Phase II of field training, or if the recruit is recycled through Phase I, or the recruit's card is punched (meaning to have their merit or credentials verified) and that recruit washes out. Let the games begin.

My advice to you: pay attention. Don't make your goal just to get through the training and pass. Your goal is to learn how to save your life and the lives of those around you. Take it seriously, because you never know when your new, exciting job will turn deadly serious.

3

THE POLICE ACADEMY, OR
HELL ON EARTH

Reminiscent of Dante's Seven Rings of Hell, the police academy is a required ring of hell for every law enforcement officer in the United States, whether you serve at the local, state, or federal level. Don't even bother to try to get around it. Some officers attend their agency's own accredited, basic police school, while others attend academies run by their respective states or accredited universities. The main difference is that state academies require that a police officer candidate be sponsored by an agency to attend, while some schools run by universities will allow anyone to attend if they can pay the tuition; however, this in no way guarantees a job upon completion. One would think that by successfully completing this particular rite of passage, a recruit would be automatically anointed into the blue brotherhood, but it's just not the case. Completing the police academy is just one step in the multistep process all trainees must pass during their probationary year, including field training and, depending on the agency, mentoring.

Law enforcement training academies vary from state to state as to the methods they employ and the subjects they cover, but a few basic tenets apply to all law enforcement training. The instructors at the training academy are there to accomplish two things. One is to ruthlessly cull the trainees who are not a good fit for the profession. The instructors are intense folks. They have all the patience, sensitivity, and compassion of sharks in a feeding frenzy, and you're the chum. For example, my physical training (PT) instructor at the police academy showed up for work every day in the dark and pulled a sled of weights up and down the Emergency Vehicle Operations Center (EVOC) driving track, I think, just for fun! Their mission, which they take quite seriously, is to separate the weak from the strong, the immoral from the moral, the unethical from the ethical, the not-so-bright person from the bright one, and the average citizen from the figure of authority in our society, the police officer.

The instructors' other mission is to tear down the well-meaning but inept individual and to rebuild in his or her place a professional law enforcement officer. Emphasis on *professional.*

The few trainees who survive the first week academy grinder can look forward to a system of checks and balances over the next eight to ten weeks that intensifies the culling process and ensures that only those best suited for police work survive. It's a brutal and often demoralizing process, but necessary.

Here's why. The academy is tough, but being a cop on the streets is exponentially tougher and is a high-stakes occupation. On the street, there exists a small, if any, margin of error for cops. The decisions that law enforcement officers make in a split second can and usually do have far-reaching consequences for victims, offenders, the agency, and the officers involved, as well as their families. Some decisions they make may literally be the difference between life and death for themselves or others.

Almost all of their decisions can mean the difference between continuing to be a law enforcement officer and being shamefully discharged from your profession and possibly facing civil or criminal charges.

This intense training is important for many reasons, such as doing your job properly and safely for all involved, knowing and abiding by the law, protecting your community, and being able to have a career that isn't cut short by your funeral.

Another reason is the fact that every decision you make may be tried in the courts, scrutinized and discussed among your department cadre and higher-ranking officials, and vehemently denounced by the media and general public ad nauseam. Everyone has 20/20 vision in hindsight and is eager to tell you and everyone else within earshot how they would have done it if they had been in your shoes.

Never mind that they were *not* in your shoes and are clueless about how the situation unfolded, the risks, the law, the 540 pages of General Orders you have to abide by, and the fact that you were at the end of your fourth ten-hour shift this week.

The paper shufflers, the television-show-trained lawyers, and the blustering cop wannabes relish every opportunity to pontificate on your shortcomings. Your every action will potentially be fodder for secret scrutiny behind closed doors by politicians, the district attorney's office, and in the court of public opinion on the six o'clock news as the media presents the story in a forty-five-second clip.

In essence, police officers have a bullseye painted on their back. Everyone from criminals with cop-killer bullets in an assault rifle, to a self-important citizen, to a coworker with a grudge and a supervisor's ear, can take a shot at them in different ways. So it's the police officer's job to keep all of them safe and happy.

It's imperative for the officers and their departments that the academy instructors produce well-rounded police officers who are knowledgeable and professional from among the ranks of those recruits who are still standing by week ten. Of course, it's impossible to turn out a veteran police officer in the short amount of time the academy staff has to work with, but it is possible to turn out a cop who is not a quitter when the going gets tough. It's possible to turn out a cop who knows basic traffic and criminal laws, a cop who can safely arrive on-scene at a call, and a cop who knows with little or no supervision what to do and can effectively do it once they get there. It's really not a mystery what goes on behind the scenes in the hallowed halls of justice.

As mentioned earlier, the first thing academy staff wants to accomplish when recruits arrive for their first week of training is to size them up and essentially see if they have what it takes to become a successful law enforcement officer. The staff accomplishes this in a number of ways. One of these is to stress the recruits' bodies and minds to the breaking point, and then push a little further.

It starts when you as a recruit arrive and file into the academy gymnasium and stand at attention behind the books and materials you will use over the next ten weeks in the classroom. If you've seen a movie about basic training in the military or have experienced it firsthand, you'll find this to be a similar experience. A lot of yelling and dressing down of recruits will take place, until finally, for the sake of the schedule, you'll be given ten minutes to grab your stuff, get it into your assigned room, get dressed in your uniform, and appear again in the academy auditorium, where the academy staff will go over the rules you'll adhere to during your stay.

The following morning, you'll be pleasantly awakened at the crack of dawn by the sounds of beating on metal garbage cans. You will be ordered to get into your PT attire and report to the gym, where you will likely exercise until you throw up at least two times, after which you'll be escorted outside, where you will start running up and down a hill at what seems like a 4 to 8 percent grade over and over again until you puke some more.

It's not uncommon for a recruit to end his or her career before it even gets started in an ambulance, exiting the academy gates. Sad as that is, the instructors are very adept at breaking the fragile recruits at the academy, where they are in reasonable safety, rather than on the street, where if they break, someone could die. The instructors turn out professional police officers who have what it takes in a time of crisis. They create officers who would stand between a hostage and a gunman; officers who may successfully fight for their life with a violent offender on the side of a rural highway; who act according to their training and then may have to endure a character assassination by the media for doing what they honestly believe was their duty.

In addition to stressing recruits mentally and physically, academy instructors separate the wheat from the chaff by pushing recruits who have an innate problem with authority or anger-management issues to their limit. Obviously, someone who represents authority must subscribe to the concept of authority (both accepting authority and being the authority) and be in control at all times.

Only an emotionally stable officer can maintain control. Officers must be confident and possess restraint in the face of those who push their buttons. The officer prone to needlessly escalating situations or to responding in a knee-jerk fashion to the big-mouthed idiot on the street will not be long for the profession of peacekeeping. It's best to send these types of recruits packing early on; the academy is the first place to do that.

In response to the academy's stress and pressure, some cowardly recruits literally sneak out of the dorm in the middle of the night, never to be seen or heard from again. Apparently, they would rather do that than to have to demonstrate the character it takes to report to the academy staff that becoming a police officer is just not for them. Good riddance! Better to deal with the bad apples now than to clean up their messes later when it could be a serious matter. No officer wants a cowardly person beside them in a crisis.

Once recruits get past the physical and mental challenges presented by the academy staff, they must confront the academic and practical obstacles. All recruits are expected to demonstrate the knowledge that has been fed to them in extended classroom sessions by way of successfully completing a written test at the end of each week.

For recruits who have been engaged in experiential (hands-on) training like defense tactics, firearms training, or emergency vehicle operations, they must physically demonstrate their proficiency in each task and meet a minimum accepted standard. If a recruit fails an academic test or practical exam once, the recruit is usually given a second chance to successfully complete it. However, if a recruit fails the same test twice, he or she is washed out or recycled to a later class, depending on the policy and procedure of the recruit's agency. My department had no policy in place allowing a recruit to be recycled. No matter where a recruit is located, if he or she washes out of the academy, that recruit might as well start looking for another job, preferably one outside of law enforcement, where lives are not hanging in the balance.

It's during a recruit's time at the academy that the indoctrination begins. By design, the slow, steady regimen of blue camaraderie imprints upon recruits that *if* they make it through the academy, and *if* they do everything right, that they will be part of a very special brotherhood (even for women). Over the years, beginning at the academy, these officers will cultivate a friendship and camaraderie that few non-law-enforcement co-workers ever seek to foster or attain. This makes sense in policing, because loyalty and unity matter when lives are on the line.

At the end of the academy class, there is usually a parting session that recruits and their families are encouraged to attend. The session is usually led by a retired or veteran police officer with at least twenty-five years of experience on the job. The session topic is police stress and covers important facts about policing in America.

My session was led by a retired Boston police officer with more than twenty years on the job in various capacities. This guy was an on-call counselor for officers involved in critical incidents and had survived several personally. He knew what he was talking about, and it was valuable information, and I should have been paying close attention, but all I heard was "blah, blah, blah" because I had a shiny new badge and was star-struck with my own perceived prestige.

So, I didn't want to hear anything negative about my new, chosen profession. I had bought the whole enchilada the academy instructors were paid to serve up, and I wasn't about to let some old guy keep me from eating it. I was such an idiot.

As best I can recall, he warned us recruits and our families that their officer husband, wife, son, or daughter who just pinned on the badge will change, and often not for the better. He said that by the second year of a police officer's career, he or she will have been forsaken and abandoned by many, if not all, friends from outside of the law enforcement community.

Building on that statistic, he said, after five years on the job, most police officers are not even recognizable to their spouses or extended family members in terms of their personality and demeanor. I didn't believe what this guy was trying to tell us. Sure, I was going to change, but for the better and if anything, that would just make my current friends idolize and worship me even more, right?

The wizened veteran cop went on to say that if a police officer contin-ues in the profession to retirement age, he or she will likely die twelve years prematurely of, take a breath here, heart disease, lung cancer, di-abetes, or cirrhosis of the liver, or in the line of duty by an offender's hand, in a car accident while responding to a call, or be run over on the side of the highway while on a traffic stop, gunned down in cold blood by a violent offender, or by committing suicide.

These are sobering facts. And they are well-documented. Many offi-cers will become alcoholics or drug addicts or both. Some will be diag-nosed with PTSD and no longer able to function as a police officer. A few may go completely in a different direction from the laws they are sworn to uphold and become corrupt or violent, ending up in prison. Nice huh? When I attended his lecture I leaned over to one of my fellow officers and said, "Shit, that won't be me, man. This guy doesn't know what he's talking about." Boy, was I wrong about that. These are things you need to seriously consider if you want to become a police officer.

Once the new academy graduates meet the requirements of their state's Peace Officer Standards and Training Commission (POST), they return to their respective departments as POST-commissioned law en-forcement officers in their state.

So, the academy teaches the police officer candidate the basics of policing. Regardless of what department you hail from in your state, theoretically, you should, after completing the academy, be able to go back home and function as a police officer. For many graduates, the academy is the beginning and end of their training. When they arrive home, they get a set of car keys and a map of their jurisdiction, and the next thing they know they're on the midnight shift, by themselves, figuratively counting ceiling tiles most of the night. I was fortunate. At my agency, I came back from the academy to a shift staffed by fifteen veteran officers every night and had the luxury of learning the ropes under these guys. Every officer should be so fortunate. Many are not and pay the price.

Not long after my graduation from the police academy, I traveled to another county in our state where one of my classmates was employed as a deputy sheriff to ride along with him on his shift and see what rural policing was like in comparison to my city beat. Wow, talk about an indoctrination into how good I had it!

What I remember most about that night (a twelve-hour shift) was responding to a domestic disturbance at a mobile home located in the middle of what many would refer to as either nowhere, or way out in the sticks. My buddy was running emergency traffic at 120 miles per hour on a windy road, driving with his knee, while he had a sandwich in one hand and his radio mic in the other. If that wasn't scary enough, our backup was a reserve deputy with little to no training, who appeared in a sheriff's department polo shirt and baseball cap, with a gun strapped to his western belt, just east of his rodeo belt buckle. He was wearing jeans and cowboy boots, and had no other equipment with him beyond that handgun. Not even a portable radio. Let's just say, I was ready to go back to my jurisdiction at the end of that night. My confidence in rural law enforcement was not at an all-time high as a result of my experience.

In summation: Take in everything everyone tells you in your training. Assume it is the gospel. Believe it. Give it serious thought. And then sit down with your loved ones to make a decision as to whether or not a law enforcement career is a good fit for you, because your decision will have a profound and permanent impact on your life and the lives of your family.

4

FIELD TRAINING

"Get out of the car. Get in on the passenger side and don't say a word, not a word," barked the FTO to the trainee who had just wrecked his new patrol car—the patrol car the FTO had been issued just two weeks prior. Frankly, the FTO's response to the accident was generous. His trainee was "vertically challenged" and despite the FTO asking him if he needed a seat cushion to see over the dash, he had refused, probably out of pride. As a result, while on a call and arriving on scene, the trainee ran over a tree stump, and then while leaving, backed up over the same stump, hooked the front bumper from underneath, and separated it from his FTO's new patrol unit.

This noncritical accident was going to necessitate a costly repair and put the vehicle out of commission for a while, and they would need to use a loaner patrol unit, which were usually the dregs of the fleet. Picture in your mind's eye a patrol car with over 150,000 hard miles on it, complete with dents, chipped and faded paint, bald tires, old emergency equipment that may or may not function when activated, no power steering or anti-lock brakes, windows that won't roll up or down, and, as an added bonus, sunflower seeds that blow out of the vents when you turn the heater or air conditioner on. Yep, the FTO was thrilled!

That said, he put his anger aside and, rather than chew out the trainee, instead told the trainee about his worst on-duty patrol accident. He used his experience to put the trainee at ease in a difficult situation, and to keep the trainee from imploding and from wasting the department's training investment. Unfortunately, the trainee eventually decided police work was not for him, but he made that decision on his own, therefore avoiding becoming a detriment to the department later in his career.

Regardless of whether or not a law enforcement recruit starts training at the police academy, in the field training program, in Limbo Week, or somewhere in between, the recruit will have to complete the field training phase at some point.

Field training provides the recruit with an opportunity to experience the reality of policing, outside of the antiseptic classroom environment, but with a safety net and a one-on-one FTO. During this phase of training, recruits are under constant scrutiny for everything they do and don't do.

Similar to police academies, field training programs vary from agency to agency and from state to state. Many consist of three to four phases during which a recruit progressively assumes more responsibility for each call or proactive response while on duty with an FTO. The FTO will instruct, mentor, and guide the recruit along the way, gradually reducing the amount of instruction provided to the recruit, while increasing time spent on evaluating the recruit's performance and suitability for the job.

If a recruit is lucky, he or she will draw an FTO like the one at the beginning of this chapter. But not all FTOs are as delighted about training recruits or even having them inside their world, their "patrol car," for twelve hours a day. Most FTOs receive a stipend (extra pay) for taking on trainees, so for many that is their sole motivation. They aren't sincerely interested in teaching trainees anything; they just take them through the basics and give them middle-of-the-road evaluation marks to pass them to the next phase and to the next FTO.

The tool used by the FTO to evaluate the trainee is commonly referred to as the daily observation report, or DOR for short. The DOR has various categories and subcategories used to evaluate the recruit's level of knowledge, performance, appearance, attitude, and relationships. A DOR is generated by the trainee's FTO for every call the trainee responds to and every proactive event initiated by the trainee. Trainees are graded in each category and subcategory on a scale of 1 to 7. A score of 1 is "Not Acceptable" and 7 is "Superior." Each DOR is supplemented by a narrative that provides the training sergeant with a written explanation for each score earned by the trainee. The goal of the FTO is to assist the trainee in successfully reaching a consistent middle ground on DORs and to ensure that if a trainee has a high potential to wash out, his or her failures are documented, supported, and legally defensible should the trainee sue the city following their separation.

Trainees live or die by the DORs they receive in field training. A succession of low-scoring DORs can result in a trainee's dismissal and the end of their career in law enforcement at the agency where they were hired, before it even starts.

In addition to the DOR, the trainee is judged on nonspecific but critical issues. Sometimes an FTO observes behavior that requires immediate action: for example, if the trainee exhibits a racist attitude on a call. If an FTO observes behavior in a trainee that requires immediate action, like the one just mentioned, it can be reported to the training sergeant and the trainee may face termination on the spot.

I remember one trainee who was participating in a baton training drill on a heavy bag. The trainees were told to issue verbal commands to the heavy bag while striking it. Commands were to include "stop resisting!" and "get back!" However, this trainee decided to ad lib with racial slurs. He was terminated as soon as the paperwork could be completed.

This leads me to an important point I tried to impress upon all of my trainees during their FTO phase: "One of the most important tools you can develop as a police officer is knowing how to talk with people." Notice I said, "Knowing how to talk with people," not "to people." Think about it: most of us don't like to be talked down to, talked around, or talked at. Nine out of ten people you communicate with as a police officer feel the same way you do. It really comes down to the old golden rule. An officer should treat everyone with the same respect and dignity that he or she would like to be treated with. If you follow that simple rule, you'll be well on your way to de-escalating tense situations rather than escalating them, ending up having to use force to gain involuntary compliance and then possibly being suspended, fired, or even sued personally.

During all phases of field training, trainees are encouraged to practice techniques like "Verbal Judo: The Gentle Art of Persuasion," a technique created by George J. Thompson, PhD, and Jerry B. Jenkins, and featured in a book by the same name. These techniques are specifically designed to aid the police in de-escalating situations and are practiced by storied departments like the LAPD, the NYPD, and the Chicago Police Department. You may think just by reading the title of Dr. Thompson and Mr. Jenkins' book that this is some kind of touchy-feely stuff that will not really work, but I can assure you from practice that it does work. I would also encourage you to change the way you think regarding the "touchy-feely techniques" espoused by psychologists and psychiatrists with a lot of time spent on researching their subjects and gathering scientific, empirical evidence that proves the effectiveness of their methods. Only a foolish officer prefers the use of force to gaining voluntary compliance through the use of verbal techniques. Yes, there is a time for everything, but it's about knowing what time is the right time to stop talking and act. That's something you'll have to learn from experience as a new officer, so keep your eyes open and learn from the veterans around you. Learn what to do and what not to do, when to do it and when not to do it. Trust me, you'll see it all if you stick around long enough.

On this subject, I loosely held to the following rule: I will ask you once, I will tell you once, and then I will act. I say "loosely," because, of course, I made exceptions based on each situation, time, and place. Here's an example.

Let's say I make a traffic stop, approach the violator's vehicle, tell him why I stopped him, and then ask for his license, registration, and proof of insurance, to which he responds, "I wasn't doing anything wrong, so I am not going to give you my license. You had no right to stop me." Well, rather than moving right to "I'm not going to ask you again, give me your license, registration, and proof of insurance," which is an implied threat that if there is a third time, there will be a resulting consequence, I might instead employ a verbal technique and make an appeal to the motorist for voluntary compliance, like, "Sir, you seem like a reasonable person and I know you've probably just got off work and are in a hurry to get home to your family. I can empathize with you in that regard. That said, in the State of Blank, when you sign your driver's license, you agree to produce that license when asked by a certified law enforcement officer. I would really like to earn your cooperation and get you home to your family as quickly as possible, but if you continue to refuse to produce your license I will have to take you into custody until such time as you can be identified and post bond. I don't want to do that and I know you don't want to be held up. So, would you please provide me with your license, registration, and proof of insurance? In return, I will do my best to expedite your return to your family."

Now, that approach may or may not work. But at least you tried to appeal to the motorist's better nature and on your unit's video and audio you come across as reasonable and patient, not as a blowhard lacking tact in what is really a common encounter with motorists who think they know more about the law and its enforcement than you do as a certified police officer.

In the end, you may have to move to step three, but you try to avoid it at all costs, because having to take someone to jail for failing to produce their driver's license when that person has a valid one really comes across to the magistrate, judicial commissioner, judge, and your fellow officers and supervisors as just a little silly and heavy handed.

The four phases of field training, Phase One, Phase Two, Phase Three, and Final Evaluation, are designed to methodically expose the trainee to the unique characteristics the job takes on as the average day progresses and the personality of the street changes. During this process, a recruit's demeanor, professionalism, temperament, aptitude, and job knowledge are assessed and taken into consideration.

You need to pay attention and soak it all in. Flying under the protective and wise wing of a training officer for a while can make the difference between you being a mediocre patrol officer and a law enforcement career professional.

If you ask any officer if working day shift in their city is the same as working midnight shift, or mids, or "graveyard," as it is often referred to, you'll find the officer's answer will be emphatically "no."

Think about the city or community in which you live. In the early morning hours, around 6 a.m., people are waking up, heading out the door for work, dropping the kids off at school, and basically getting their day started. Traffic inbound to your city's business district is picking up and the city's population is growing to include workers who commute from other communities.

Business owners may be discovering that their shop was burglarized overnight, homeowners may be finding items missing from their cars, and almost certainly motorists will be violating traffic laws, be involved in accidents, or both. The day-shift officers are slammed, traveling from call to call and praying for a lull in the action to grab a cup of coffee and a bagel.

Let's say, for instance, your city or community has a daytime population of one hundred thousand with only six to twelve officers available to handle all their calls for service. These numbers do not even allow for the officers who are tied up by engaging in proactive enforcement like ticket writing or checking on businesses.

By mid-morning, your city will probably have doubled or tripled its population. While rush hour is coming to an end, the report calls are just starting to pick up for the day shift. They'll take reports for everything from burglaries that occurred overnight, to fraud, employee theft, missing persons, vandalism, and the list just keeps on growing.

As the report calls begin to slow down around 11 a.m. to 1 p.m., pedestrian traffic and vehicle traffic picks up again. Calls for service increase to include everything from issues similar to the morning rush hour to fight calls at the local fast food restaurant because someone has been waiting in the drive-thru for twenty-nine minutes to receive their double cheeseburger. They are frustrated and angry that they are going to be late getting back to the office. Their anger escalates and explodes into an assault on a fast-food worker, road rage, or a motor vehicle accident, as the enraged and hungry motorist wheels around traffic like he's at the Indy 500 on his way back to work.

By the early afternoon, average-citizen activity slows down; workers are now snug in their office or sitting like zombies in a conference room meeting, or they fall asleep under the fluorescent lights with full tummies.

Meanwhile, out on the street, day-shift officers try to grab a quick bite. Then it hits. Three short tones on their portable radios clearing the airways for emergency traffic terminate the officers' peaceful meal.

What is emergency traffic? It can be any toned-out call requiring a code 3 (lights and sirens) response. For example, a bank robbery has just occurred downtown and the first officers arrive on scene with the suspects still in the bank. The suspects have barricaded themselves inside the bank and are holding a teller hostage at gunpoint. Every available patrol unit drops what it's doing, including eating lunch, and races code 3 to the scene to provide assistance and set up a perimeter around the bank. The SWAT (Special Weapons and Tactics) team is activated and hostage negotiators are called in, but none of these specialized teams will arrive on scene for forty-five minutes. There's nothing for the dedicated resources to do but wait and be prepared to respond if the suspects start behaving badly, like shooting innocent people.

Meanwhile, if any citizens have broken down in traffic, been involved in a motor vehicle accident, or have an offense report to file, they're just going to have to wait.

Now it's about 3 p.m. and the evening shift is about to come on duty. Following roll call, they'll have to take the place of officers already on scene at the bank robbery, handle evening rush hour, and try to eat dinner before the typical evening calls for service start stacking up in the dispatchers' queues. Between the end of rush hour and the end of evening shift at 1 a.m. the following morning, evening-shift officers will respond to calls ranging from domestic violence, public intoxication, and fighting to lost children and driving under the influence. Around 9 p.m., the midnight shift will be coming on and for four hours, both evening shift and midnight shift officers enjoy a four-hour overlap, during which they have double the resources and personnel allocated.

By the time evening shift punches the clock and heads out the door for home, the city is once again changing. The business district is empty, most commuters have arrived home in the 'burbs, and it's time for the crazies to make their nightly appearance. Every strange, weird, high, homeless, or strung-out character starts popping out from the woodwork, and it's up to the midnight shift officers to make sure these people don't escape into the general population and wreak some kind of havoc. Most of these folks we know by name and refer to as our "frequent flyers." They're the ones who we arrest over and over again. Nine times out of ten we can't even engage them in conversation before we are rolling around on the ground.

They go by and answer to cute little monikers like Bebe, Dap Daddy, Little Bubba, Squirrel Baby, Go Ray, and many others too numerous to mention here. You may encounter one of these upstanding citizens anywhere and doing just about anything. You may find one such person defecating behind the dumpster at the corner convenience store. Or you may encounter someone like one of our frequent flyers, walking down the center line of Main Street with a vodka bottle balanced on his head, a Bible in one hand, and a broom handle (makeshift staff) in the other. He believes that he is Moses parting the Red Sea.

Television shows like *Reno 911* are hysterical to the general public and law enforcement officers alike, because they are only separated from the reality of policing by one or two degrees. Every agency has a Lt. Dangle, a Trudy Wygle, and an Officer Garcia. Just change the names, and you have yourself a police agency in any city.

At the end of Phase Three and twelve weeks of field training across three very different shifts, recruits return to the shift of their primary FTO for Final Evaluation. This is where the rubber meets the road. It's time for recruits to demonstrate what they have learned. If a recruit cannot handle himself or herself on the street by now, it's probably not going to happen.

Now, the recruit reports to duty in full uniform and for all intents and purposes, the recruit is solo. The primary FTO reports to shift in plain clothes (civilian attire), in order to put the focus on the recruit, rides shotgun with the recruit and evaluates him or her on everything the recruit does from the beginning of shift to the end of shift on the all-important DOR. The recruit is not allowed to ask the FTO for assistance or advice, and the FTO may only engage the recruit or citizen if an emergency situation arises or an officer safety issue becomes apparent.

The recruit does have a few fallbacks, however. Recruits can always ask for assistance or guidance from a non-FTO or backup officer on scene. They may also reach out for a supervisor such as a shift sergeant or shift lieutenant. Nonetheless, reaching out for help should be the last resort for a recruit. If the recruit relies too heavily on peers or supervisors for support, that deficit will be reflected in the DOR.

If the recruit completes the Final Evaluation with acceptable marks on the DORs, depending on the agency's policies and procedures, the recruit will be placed on his or her own to patrol and answer calls solo. Recruits with unacceptable marks may be recycled through part or all of their previous training. In a worst-case scenario, such recruits may be terminated. Keep in mind that a retained recruit will still be on probation for the remaining six months of his or her first year and subject to dismissal at any time during that period with little or no cause. What's more, many agencies do not allow their new officers to join the Fraternal Order of Police (FOP) or Police Benevolent Association (PBA) until after the successful completion of their probationary year. So, recruits do not enjoy the benefit of a State Legal Defense Fund or an attorney on retainer in the event that they get themselves in trouble. This is important, because in this job, every day you report for duty and hit the street, you can count on trouble of some sort. From the time an officer punches in, it's only a matter of minutes before trouble comes knocking. An officer's career longevity light either remains bright or starts to grow dim based largely on how that officer and his or her peers respond to any given situation. For more about liability and the police officer, see chapter 6.

5

CONGRATULATIONS! YOU'VE EARNED A SPOT AT THE BOTTOM

"Hey, welcome to the shift, err, ah, what's your name again?" When you've completed your six-month stint in training and have finally been assigned to your second, or more likely, your third choice of shift assignments, no one will know your name. And guess what? No one wants to!

There are several reasons no one wants to know your name and let's start with the obvious one. No one knows you, or more importantly, no one knows who you are as a person or who you will be as a police officer. Until they've had a chance to see you in action and the results, no one wants to.

Cops don't trust easily or often, not even their own. Don't believe me? The next time you see cops eating at a fast-food restaurant, take a look to see if their backs are against a wall where they can see all the doors and people in the restaurant. I think you'll be surprised about what you find. There exists a protective wall or curtain around all police officers, and they aren't going to let it down for just anyone, especially an unproven probationary officer. The unknown can "get you jammed up!" Yep, that is an official cop metaphor employed to describe an uncomfortable situation you've been placed in, usually by someone else and through no fault of your own. That situation has the potential to affect you personally, professionally, or both in an adverse way.

Another reason no one wants to know you or be your best buddy is they don't know how long you're going to be around, figuratively or literally. Let's face it, in this line of work you could lose your life stepping out the back door of the station after roll call. Unfortunately, some officers have. Also a lot of rookies find out, usually within their first year, that this job of being a police officer is not for them, or their spouse tells them, "This job is not for you"; that is, you'd better find another job or you'll be finding another spouse.

I knew an FTO once upon a time who trained a female recruit who was a college graduate, physically fit, almost six feet tall, endowed with common sense, and intellectually very smart. In short, she was going to be a great cop—at least that's what her FTO thought and told the rest of us veteran officers out of her earshot. Let's call her Susan.

Susan and her FTO responded to a domestic disturbance in progress one night while assigned to second shift. I'll set the scene for you. The call came out on the radio shortly after nine o'clock on a spring evening. The dispatcher advised that a male subject was chasing his girlfriend through the backyards of a public housing complex and knocking her to the ground with a football tackle every time he would get close enough to her. She would fight her way free and then keep on running, trying to get away from him. By the time Susan and her FTO got there another unit had already arrived, caught both parties, and separated them in an attempt to ascertain just what was going on. By this time, the female subject's pants had already been literally ripped off of her body and she was standing by a patrol car partially clothed. Susan was assigned to speak with her since she was in a state of undress, while her FTO and another officer stood on either side of the male suspect, who was told to sit on the front bumper of a patrol car, a position of disadvantage should he decide to "break bad" or "buck up," two cop terms for becoming aggressive and noncompliant.

After a little investigation, it became clear that the male suspect was the primary aggressor and as such (as required by state law) would be arrested and transported to the county jail. When that time came, the suspect, who was drunk and pretty stout for a little guy, decided he did not want to go to lockup. An officer can usually tell when a suspect is going to resist arrest, because the offender usually telegraphs it in some way; suspects ball up their fists, take off their coat, or tense up as soon as you put your hands on them to effect the arrest. The latter was the case this time. Remember, Susan is in a position to watch this process go down, standing nearby with the female subject.

As soon as the suspect resisted, he was arm barred and taken to the ground by the veteran officers in an attempt to take him into custody without anyone getting hurt. Not surprisingly, the suspect didn't want to put his hands behind his back once he was on the ground for the officers to handcuff him. So one of the officers unholstered his Taser, removed the cartridge housing the fish-hook-like probes with twenty-five-foot leads, and then performed a drive stun with the Taser's exposed contacts to the body of the suspect, verbally ordering him to put his hands behind his back. That did the trick and the handcuffs went on.

The officers picked the suspect up off of the ground and escorted him to the rear door of the FTO's patrol unit. Predictably, the suspect didn't want to get in and placed his left leg in the rear door jamb in an attempt to keep the officers from getting him into the back seat and closing the door, which would mean game over for the suspect, at least theoretically.

The officers gained the suspect's compliance with a few knees to the thigh of the suspect, and in he went.

After the call, the FTO observed that Susan was uncharacteristically quiet for the rest of the shift, even though they had reviewed the incident, deconstructing it step-by-step to ensure that Susan understood what happened, how it happened, why it happened, the techniques employed by the veteran officers, and so on.

When Susan arrived the next day for the start of her shift, she wasn't in uniform and had all of her gear in her duty bag. Suffice it to say, Susan decided that this job, being a police officer, wasn't for her and that she was not comfortable having to employ the tactics she observed the previous night.

The moral of the story is simply this. When a training officer (FTO) says, "This job (being a police officer) isn't for everyone," he isn't saying it to discourage the recruit. He's just reminding the trainee that it's okay to evaluate how you feel about the job while you're in training, and if you decide it's not for you, there's no shame in admitting it and moving on.

Veteran officers don't want to get too close to new officers because they don't want to waste an investment in friendship or personal feelings on a newbie. Most officers who have been around a few years have already lost friends in the line of duty and attended more funerals than they would care to remember. If they don't invest in a new officer emotionally, they don't have to care if something happens to that officer or be invested beyond wearing a black mourning band over their badge for a few days. It's just easier. And easy is what you want when the majority of what you do every day is physically and emotionally draining.

Let me give you another extreme example. There was a new officer on the force once who responded to a fight call in progress between several high-school kids on a school bus. This officer was a piece of work, and that is putting it mildly. When the second and third officer arrived on-scene, traffic was already at a standstill in every direction due to the bus having been stopped in the middle of the roadway. The bus driver and several students were still engaged in a mêlée inside the bus, and the new officer, who had nicknamed himself "Bad Guy," was standing outside of the bus smoking a cigarette while reclined against a telephone pole.

The backup officers passed "Bad Guy" on their way into the bus to put a stop to the fight, asking him over their shoulder, "What the hell are you doing?" which is to say "not doing." Once order had been restored and the young hellions were handcuffed in the back of the squads, the winded officers asked "Bad Guy" why he had stood there smoking a cigarette instead of intervening or helping them quell the situation. "Bad Guy" responded with "Hey, that's not my job." That was "Bad Guy's" last day on the job.

That brings us to the topic of being invisible. A recruit should strive, figuratively speaking, to be invisible. The more you're seen as a new officer and the less you're heard from, the better. First of all, you learn more when you quietly observe experienced officers doing the job you are aspiring to do. Second, it's highly unlikely that anything you could offer to the commentary would be a value add. It's more likely that what you have to say is wrong, already been said, or just plain stupid, and none of those are beneficial. Finally, if you're invisible, you're less likely to receive a complaint stemming from something you said or did because you didn't know any better. Fewer complaints result in a higher likelihood that you will survive your probationary year and actually have the opportunity to become the police officer you want to be so badly.

As a new officer, chances are your starting salary will be just barely enough to feed you and pay your rent and utilities, assuming your privately owned vehicle (POV) is already paid for, you are not married, and you don't have any expensive vices like drinking, womanizing, gambling, alimony, or child support, or any combination of those aforementioned issues. You'll be working at night and sleeping during the day. You won't know if you're coming or going for quite a while, and on your wonderful days off, Tuesday and Wednesday, you'll be in traffic court, general sessions court, grand jury, or circuit court. You'd better hope your assigned court day is Wednesday. If it's Tuesday, you will be up for up to twenty-four hours before you see home again.

When you do finally get home, you should be exhausted and ready to get some much needed and well-earned sleep. Unfortunately for you, you'll have three voicemail messages to return, your e-mail inbox will be overflowing with mail from friends and relatives who want to know why they never get to see you anymore, and your spouse or significant other will want to discuss what color curtains you think will match the new carpet best, what you want to eat for dinner, and why you're not emotionally present in your relationship. There will likely be a stack of unopened mail by the door, mostly bills that will need your immediate attention. When you're finished with all that, your checkbook balance should be about five dollars.

And that leads us to the final topic of this chapter. Hey, where did all my friends go? Believe me when I say it's not rocket science. When you become a police officer, you become a public servant in the literal sense of the term. Your life is no longer your own. It belongs to the job and the people you serve, twenty-four hours a day, seven days a week. Okay, you might try deluding yourself by subscribing to the old "I leave my work at the office" cliché, but you and I both know it's not true and so does everyone else.

Additionally, you spend so much time at work or thinking about work that it's all you ever talk about. At first it's cool, because everyone watches *COPS* and wants to live vicariously through your war stories. But after a while, it's boring and depressing. Officers spend so much time dealing with people whose lives are in the toilet or are about to be that they have this negative vibe about them. I know I go out with my friends to forget about work and the reality of life. I don't want to hear some burned-out guy I support through my taxes complain about a job that will set him up with a pension after twenty-five years, in addition to his 401k and Social Security benefits.

When you do have some free time, you had better spend it with your family, because in the end, they're the only ones who will take care of you when you can't do it for yourself anymore.

6

LIABILITY IN POLICING

Liability!

Listen, if you only remember one word from this book, this one should be it. We live in a litigious society. If you doubt that, all you have to do is turn on your five o'clock news program and you'll become a believer.

One of the officers I often rode with during the mentoring phase of my probationary year was fond of stating, tongue-in-cheek, the word "liability" every time we were rehashing a contentious or potentially problematic call that we had just handled. He also encouraged me to make sure I documented every action where "liability" could become an issue, in great detail and with a high level of accuracy, and to go a step further. He encouraged me to keep my own set of files separate from the police department containing this documentation, as paper trails tend to have a way of going missing, mysteriously, when a lawsuit is initiated, someone is exposed, or both.

This was sound advice imparted by a veteran officer, and it was wisdom I took seriously and passed on to my trainees years later.

There can be no doubt that engaging in policing and its activities will expose you to liability on a daily basis. Even if you, the officer, do everything right, someone can still claim the opposite and drag you and the department into an unfounded and frivolous lawsuit that will hang over you and the department, cost your agency a great deal of money to defend, cost you personally, and maybe even lead, in a worst case scenario, to the economic downfall of your family and the ones that you love.

If you want to protect yourself from this, there are ways to do it, and I suggest you look into them sooner rather than later. One of the easiest and most cost-effective steps you can take is to join your local chapter of the Fraternal Order of Police or Police Benevolence Association at the conclusion of your probationary year or before if your agency allows it. While police officers are forbidden by law to organize in a union, these associations advocate and lobby on behalf of law enforcement professionals on the local, state, and national level. Additionally, they both offer and maintain legal defense funds that you can contribute to and avail yourself of if you are sued in the line of duty personally or if the department wiggles its way out of the lawsuit and leaves you holding the ball.

The only catch here is that you have to apply to use the funds from the FOP and PBA's legal defense funds when you want to draw on them. They have the right to deny your application. Also, if you win your civil suit or countersue and are awarded damages, you will have to pay the money you borrowed for your defense back to your association. Those considerations aside, it's kind of like purchasing an umbrella insurance policy from a reputable company. Now, I know what you're thinking. Could I also purchase an insurance policy from a commercial carrier? After all, better to have too much coverage than not enough; right? Well, the answer is emphatically yes. The cost associated with a policy that will cover you for up to one million dollars could range anywhere from seven to twenty-two dollars per month, not too much to pay for peace of mind. So at the risk of sounding like an insurance agent, which I am not, I would suggest you look into it and give it serious consideration.

There was a convenience store in a neighborhood I patrolled that was positioned on the corner of a street. I wouldn't call it a "bad" neighborhood, because there are good people and positive qualities in every community and it's not fair to paint everyone with a broad brush. So let's just say we frequently responded to calls in the area.

This particular convenience store was a favorite target for foot traffic and shoplifting. A lot of foot traffic in a neighborhood is often a sign of economic disadvantage, which can create an environment where people are desperate and commit crimes against property, persons, or both as a result. So, back to the market. Over a short span of time, it had been hit for small items like cigars, cigarettes, beer, and so on, as there was usually only one clerk on duty and if that clerk became distracted, it was easy

for a suspect to lift an item. The good news is that the store had cameras that worked and it didn't take long to establish suspects.

We had a team of plainclothes officers, a Flex (short for flexible) Unit, whose job it was to respond to specific problems around the city with targeted enforcement in hopes of preventing, slowing down, or stopping crime. One night, this unit positioned officers in the stock room of this particular convenience store. The officers in the stockroom were assigned to watch the security cameras. Additionally, there were "catch" officers outside of the store and out of plain view to stop, investigate, and arrest any shoplifters as their description was radioed in from the officers inside of the store. Kind of a tag-team effort.

A pattern of behavior had been established at this location, complete with a general time frame and the usual suspects. And, sure enough, the suspects showed up around the appointed time and lifted a pack of cigars that was probably worth less than five dollars.

The officers secreted in the stock room observed the misdemeanor take place, and then the catch officers attempted to effect an arrest when the suspects passed the point of purchase without paying for the cigars; that is, they passed the cash register and left the building through the front doors. The officers outside of the store appeared, identified themselves, and attempted what is commonly referred to as a stop, frisk, halt to satisfy their reasonable suspicion and establish their probable cause to arrest the suspects for shoplifting.

Unfortunately, the suspects did not comply with the officers' verbal commands and instead decided to commit another misdemeanor: resisting stop, frisk, halt. Yep, they ran. The officers gave chase on foot through the neighborhood, over fences, around blind corners, through backyards and through the houses of complete strangers (in through the back door and out through the front door), ending in the living room of the suspect's domicile (residence).

Now, I'm sure you are asking yourself the question, could the officers lawfully pursue the suspect into his house without a warrant? The answer is yes! This foot chase falls under a legal term referred to as "Hot Pursuit." This means that the officers are pursuing a suspect immediately following a crime (in this case, a misdemeanor committed in the presence of the officers). "Hot Pursuit" is an exception to laws governing unlawful search and seizure. Therefore the officers had a legal right to pursue the suspect into his house and a lawful right to seize him and "arrest him" without a warrant because the crime occurred in their presence and imme-diately before the pursuit. Nothing is ever as simple as it seems on the surface, and this is why armchair quarterbacks watching the local news often criticize the actions of officers without understanding the law or laws governing their actions or the circumstances surrounding the event. No understanding of the law and no direct knowledge of the event will often lead to a lack of understanding on the part of the public and the incident being taken out of context.

Okay, back to our story. At the termination of the pursuit and follow-ing the arrest, during which the suspect was handcuffed and leaned up against a recliner while sitting on the floor, the suspect complained of pain in his chest (having a heart attack). The officers immediately called for EMS (ambulance and fire department first responders) to attend to the suspect and in the meantime provided aid to the suspect within their ability and training.

I know you must be thinking at this point, "Those officers subjected the suspect or suspects to a wild and unnecessary foot chase through a residential neighborhood that ultimately culminated in the suspect having a heart attack due to overexertion." Well, if I were making the case against the officers in a civil lawsuit, I might represent the incident that way. But in reality, the suspect was an avid drug user, had been using drugs immediately before committing the crime, had compromised his cardiac health by using drugs on this and many previous occasions, and had a history of a heart condition. These are circumstances the officers had no reasonable way of knowing or ascertaining prior to the com-mencement of the foot pursuit. Furthermore, if the suspect had complied with the officers' verbal commands to stop when he was caught, the foot pursuit never would have started, the suspect would not have overexerted himself, and he would not have been as likely to suffer a heart attack; this is what I would argue if I were the defense attorney for the officers.

Unfortunately for the officers and the department, the suspect died from the heart attack while in custody, a death which resulted from dam-age caused by drug use over an extensive period of time leading up to and during the commission of a crime. So guess what? The officers and the department were sued by the family of the suspect.

That brings us full circle to where we started this chapter. While the officers were not criminally liable for their actions and the death of the suspect, they and their agency were sued. And while the officers and the department won the suit and were acquitted of any civil responsibility, negligence, or wrongdoing in the end, they were still subjected to years of litigation and expense, personally and professionally. I hope they had insurance. What was that word again? Liability! Remember it!

7

FINANCES, HEALTH, AND THE POLICE OFFICER

When you sign up to become a law enforcement officer, you are signing up to be a public servant. Make no mistake about it. I started with a base salary of $31,000 annually; pretty lean in terms of remuneration for services provided in the twenty-first century, but not where policing is concerned. It's actually a better starting salary than many agencies in the United States provide.

As a police officer, you will not be allowed to engage in outside employment during your probationary year, and in most cases, not even after probation. Why? Well, enforcing the law requires, in the minds of most governments, all of your available energy and much of your time. Again, you are a "public servant" and expected to sacrifice as such. You have given your life to this pursuit: law enforcement.

But once you've completed your probationary year, chances are you'll be able to work extra jobs (special assignments) when you are off duty that come through the police department. These jobs are paid by the hour and usually pay pretty well, but will have to be performed after your shift or on your day/s off, and will usually be capped at twenty hours per week. This way everyone has a chance to work one and no one overdoes it. The assignments can range from providing security for people or property and special events. They can also involve directing traffic for construction projects, or escorting vehicles, and so on. When I was an officer, I had the opportunity to provide security for celebrities such as Kid Rock, Tim McGraw, and Bonnie Bramlett (half of the 1970s duo Delaney and Bonnie) who toured and performed with Eric Clapton. So it is possible to supplement your income and provide a better standard of living for yourself and your family, but the trade-off is more time away from your loved ones and less rest. Plus, you need to know that sustaining this on a regular basis is not usually possible. Sometimes the extra jobs dry up, and sometimes you're just too tired to work them.

Another source of extra income or savings can come from your living arrangement. Some apartment complexes and condo communities will provide you with a place to live rent-free or at a discounted rate, but in return you have to respond to disturbances in the complex as the "courtesy officer," on and off duty. You'll also have to ensure the premises are secure every night, and you may have to lock the pool, clubhouse, and offices daily.

There is one other source of income that will likely be afforded to you on an "as-needed basis," and that is the opportunity to work overtime hours by extending your workday into the next shift. Occasionally, when officers become ill or there is an emergency that prevents them from working their scheduled shift, the shift supervisor of the shift that is short on personnel may offer you the opportunity to work overtime on the next shift. Again, there is a limit as to how much of this you can do physically, and these occasions are irregular at best. This is a source of income you cannot count on, just like extra jobs.

That said, look into your agency's policy regarding extra jobs, discounted housing, and overtime. If you can save what you earn, you will find yourself with a nice nest egg to draw on when you need it.

It's summer in America, the month of August, and on this day there's not a cloud in the sky; it's one hundred degrees in the shade, with a heat index of 115, 98 percent humidity, and you are standing in the middle of the interstate directing traffic at a multicar accident, where the temperature on the pavement is 136 degrees. You are wearing a dark blue or black uniform, with a thirty-pound duty belt in patent leather strapped around your waist, and you're also wearing a Kevlar bulletproof vest underneath your uniform shirt, boots that come up above your ankles, and a hat that holds in the heat with a shiny badge right in the center of it. What do you have? A recipe for heat exhaustion if you are out there for very long, and if you are just starting to drink water and are not already hydrated, it's too late! Your next stop will likely be the emergency room, where they will fill you up with IV fluids, some type of pediatric electrolyte drink, and give you an IV pain reliever for the awful migraine headache you will have. You will be so messed up that your body will literally convulse and shake, because essentially, when you hit the door of the ER, you were only one step away from heat stroke.

Yes, there are dangers in policing that have nothing to do with facing threats from a suspect. There are significant dangers to your health and you need to be prepared for them, and proactively work to avoid them.

Besides all the damage you can do to your body through self-medication in an attempt to deal with job-related stressors and conflict at home and in your personal life, you, the new police officer, also need to be concerned with other health threats you will be exposed to in a law enforcement career. What are these? Well, we've covered heat exhaustion and self-inflicted damage, but there are others, such as not eating well (consuming too much convenience food, eating too fast, eating too much or not enough), back problems due to sitting for long periods of time in your patrol car on a duty belt, problems with your feet because you stand for a long time on concrete over and over again, disruption to your circadian sleep cycle because you're on a shift rotation and work odd hours, damage to your hearing because you are exposed to loud noises on a regular basis (like sirens, discharging of firearms and munitions, equipment operation while working extra jobs or traffic control), compromised vision due to low-light exposure and exposure to bright light (MAG and LED lights, strobe lights, colored light, no light, headlights), not to mention eye strain from looking at a mobile data terminal, your cell phone, and other backlit devices too long. Also, let's not forget damage to your liver from nonprescription pain relievers you take for headaches and backaches, potential damage to your lungs from inhaling smoke from fires (vehicles, homes, and commercial buildings that contain toxins) and secondhand cigarette smoke in enclosed areas you are called to (trailers, bars, houses), and exposure to pepper spray, tear gas, smoke from burning gunpowder at the firing range, and the chemicals you use to clean your patrol car after someone vomits, urinates, defecates, or does all three inside it.

Also, let's not forget that many of the people you deal with are not the most savory individuals. Many of them have diseases that are communicable, like HIV, Hepatitis B, or tuberculosis. You'll need to be vaccinated against these to the extent possible because you never know when a suspect will spit or cough in your face, throw something at you or on you, or you'll be stuck with a needle or some other sharp object when searching a vehicle or premises, even with gloves. You should also be current on your tetanus shot in the event you are cut with an edged weapon, like a dirty kitchen knife, or receive a wound as a result of some accident while at work, like inadvertently stepping on something sharp that penetrates your boot and injures your foot.

So how can you avoid these health risks and ensure your physical well-being to the extent you are able? Well, start by packing your own lunch and committing to healthy food choices. Exercise every day, in all of your free time. Get as much sleep and rest as possible without using sleep aids like diphenhydramine (Benadryl, ZzzQuil). Drink water and sports drinks with no carbonation to stay hydrated regularly. Wear sunglasses that block ultraviolet rays. Get a cool pack to put inside your vest and a cop-cooling system (basically a vacuum hose that hooks up to the air-conditioning vent in your patrol car) that you can insert between your bulletproof vest and your body to lower your core body temperature on a hot day. Wear good boots or shoes with arch support that breathe well. Stay current on your inoculations. Attend regular checkups with your general practitioner. Avoid running the heat in your patrol car all day or night in the winter, as this will dry out your sinuses and can lead to sinus infections and dehydration. Wear hearing protection when you are on the firing (gun) range or working an extra job around heavy equipment. Wear leather or Kevlar gloves to avoid needle sticks or cuts due to contact with sharp objects.

These are just a few of the ways you can increase the likelihood that your health will not be as adversely affected by your job than if you did not take these precautions. Notice what I said there, "as" adversely affected. Make no mistake, you will suffer physically despite your best efforts to prevent it. All officers do, because keeping up with preventative measures will become harder and harder the farther you go into your career as a result of aging, prolonged exposure, and less and less time to devote to staying healthy. The day will come—mark my words—where you will be doing good just to get four to six hours sleep every day, or night, as the case may be.

You owe it to yourself and your family to seriously consider these issues before making the decision to pursue a career in law enforcement.

8

COMMUNICATIONS AND INTER-AGENCY COOPERATION

At its base, police communications or dispatch is responsible for answering phone calls (incoming calls for service), prioritizing, and then routing those assignments to officers on patrol, firefighters, and emergency medical personnel via radio and mobile data terminals. Referring to dispatchers or communications officers as multitaskers would be a gross understatement. They have a very difficult and stressful job, maybe even more stressful than the job of the first responders they coordinate.

As previously mentioned, communications officers don't just coordinate the response of police officers, they coordinate the response of firefighters, emergency medical services, mutual aid agencies, and more. At the same time, they're dealing with radio and phone traffic, both incoming and outgoing, and answering text messages and calls from officers' cell phones, text messages via mobile data terminals, 911 lines, and alarm services. Some agencies use ten codes to help streamline radio traffic and also encrypt information that criminals monitoring police radio traffic with a scanner might be able to hear and use. That said, with changes in technology and the move from analog radio bands to digitally secure bands, many agencies are transitioning from the use of ten codes to plain talk when communicating over radios. Plain talk is just what it sounds like, and it not only simplifies understanding, but makes it possible for mutual aid agencies that use different ten-code systems to more easily and effectively communicate across boundaries.

Communication is just starting once communications officers have dispatched the necessary first responders. They will monitor the first responders' progress to the location of the call for service, answer first responders' questions while on the way, continue to communicate with the caller and forward information updates to first responders, and handle all communications and requests once the first responders arrive on scene until they clear the location they have responded to and ended the call for service with a status.

What's more, they monitor that radio traffic and are exposed to horrific sounds emanating from victims, cries for help, officers' distress calls, and more—all without the ability to take any direct action to help beyond communication and coordination of resources. Imagine how frustrating that would be. All the more exasperating because you know the first responders intimately. Usually, the dispatcher or communications officer has worked with them for years. They know them so well that they can recognize their voice over the radio without hearing their call sign. They know when they are calm, when they are nervous, and when they are in trouble and need help. To call it a difficult job would be an understatement. So, you'd think their emotional well-being and health would be monitored and assistance would be made available just like the services offered to police officers and other first responders, right? Wrong.

The needs of communications personnel are often overlooked, and the resources for them are frequently limited if offered at all. Pretty incredible, considering that dispatchers are literally the first responders' lifeline. Because of that fact, first responders should maintain really good relationships with their communications personnel. Angering a dispatcher could result in a first responder being dispatched to really lousy calls and keep him or her running all over the city from the beginning of the shift to the end of the shift. It could also result in a slow response of backup and ancillary services when a first responder needs them most. Now, I'm sure you're thinking that a communications officer or dispatcher would be more professional than that, and you're generally right. But keep in mind, they're human and vulnerable to the same prejudices, grudges, and ill feelings that all of us are.

So, keep them happy. They're stuck in that communications center for the duration of their shift. Bring them takeout, run errands for them when things are slow in the field, and take advantage of every opportunity to make their job easier. Your job as a first responder will be easier as a result.

One of the greatest advancements in policing in America is undoubtedly an increased level of inter-agency cooperation that has been created through the advent of technology. These technologies and ways to share information locally and globally take on many forms, not the least of which is fusion centers dedicated to the facilitation of inter-agency cooperation. These centers exist virtually, on the Internet, and literally, in large, terraced situation rooms not unlike a stadium-style movie theater. What's more, these fusion centers are staffed by local, state, and federal officers, information technology professionals, and emergency management agencies. They are ready to coordinate resources and provide necessary and real-time information to assist law enforcement in its response to natural disasters, criminal investigations, domestic and international terrorism, and critical incidents. And they are prepared to assist agencies at the outset, during, and after these events have taken place.

So who organizes and funds these efforts? Well, truthfully, the funding comes from a variety of sources. From the federal government, to state and local agencies' budgets, and even private donors. Oversight and organization usually emanates from the federal government or state governments, who reach out to local agencies for inclusion. Suffice it to say, these centers embody a real team effort.

Through these fusion centers, a detective can obtain a comprehensive, detailed report on a person's entire life, from finances, to civil and criminal records, to what kind of car that person drives, who his or her cell phone carrier is, and even photographs and fingerprints. You can imagine how useful this information is to investigators and criminal profilers. Of course, this information is guarded by the fusion center, and law enforcement agencies or officers wishing to access it must submit a verbal and a written request justifying why they need it and what they are specifically seeking. Law enforcement is held accountable for the information it receives and how it is utilized, and what happens to it once it's been consumed.

Aside from the advent of the fusion center, law enforcement agencies cooperate in other ways. For example, patrol cars are equipped with radios that are programmed with the frequencies of neighboring agencies to make it easier to communicate in evolving situations where jurisdictional boundaries are crossed rapidly. County jails house prisoners whose status is either pre- or postconviction for agencies that are too small to operate a holding facility or jail. Additionally, local, county, state, and federal officers conduct special operations together to apprehend many criminals involved in drug and theft rings, often referred to as round-ups, stings, and sweeps. And it goes without saying that officers from these agencies back each other up in an impromptu fashion on the street when it appears that the situation is lopsided or even. Cops like to have the upper hand, and that often comes in the form of numbers. You know the old cliché, "You (the criminal or combatant) may win the battle, but you will not win the war."

All of this happens because agencies understand and realize the value of cooperation to effectively perform what is already a difficult task faced on a daily basis: keeping the peace and protecting people who cannot defend themselves.

9

WELCOME TO YOUR NEW OFFICE

A police officer's patrol car is his or her office, whether it's a Chevy Lumina, Chevy Caprice, Chevy Impala, Ford Crown Victoria, Dodge Charger, or something more exotic like a Harley-Davidson motorcycle, a Chevy Camaro, Ford Mustang, an SUV, or even a turbocharged Volvo.

What you'll find under the hood of these vehicles varies depending on the mission of the agency. The highway patrol, the city, the sheriff's department, the campus police, the airport police, and the military police all use different vehicles or variations on the same vehicles. Some engines are small and fuel-efficient, some are large and turbocharged for pursuit on interstate systems, and some are even electric. Some are designed for cold-weather applications or rough terrain, while others are specifically designed for hot areas where sand and saltwater are present. Today, most police-package vehicles that are built by major manufacturers are equipped with hidden computers that record speed, braking, and air-bag deployments, and that information can be downloaded by motorpool personnel in the event of an at-fault accident, high-speed pursuit, or complaint involving a police officer.

On the roof of the police vehicle you'll often find a light bar that contains flashing strobes, LEDs, take-down lights, and alley lights. In the grill you'll find more alternating lights, corner strobe lights, and headlights that are referred to as "wig-wags" when operating as emergency equipment due to their flashing pattern. You'll find more strobes and LEDs at the rear bumper, including corner strobes in the taillights and even strobes on the license plate frame.

Inside the patrol unit officers will find everything needed to do the job, save for what they carry on their person. Everything is housed in its proper place in that patrol unit. Some of the common things you'll find include: a gear bag with all of the officer's paperwork, complete with a metal or plastic clipboard that holds the officer's traffic citations; a police radio; scanner; radar unit (portable and fixed); a cabin light (often red or green so that the officer can see what's going on outside of the patrol unit while completing paperwork, which is necessary as the map light is often disabled to prevent officers being lit up when they open their door on a call or traffic stop); a gun lock overhead or in the center of the cabin with a shotgun, high-powered rifle, or both; a console with buttons and knobs for the operation of emergency equipment (lights, sirens, public address system); a video unit to record what the officer and suspect say and do, also documenting the unit number, date, and time of the activity; and an emergency response bag that usually contains items like flexi-cuffs, extra ammo for every weapon the officer carries and different weapons his fellow officers carry, extra magazines for weapons, and items like a quick-clot patch in the event that an officer is shot, a flashlight, and an emergency vest.

There is a cage that separates the officer from a suspect they are transporting or detaining and they come in a variety of shapes and sizes. Some are steel, some are Plexiglas, some are solid, some have a sliding window, and some are half steel and half Plexiglas.

In the back seat of the car, door handles, window controls, and buttons for locking mechanisms have been removed for obvious reasons, and there are usually microphones and video cameras to record what a suspect says. There are seatbelts, and very often the seat is molded plastic or vinyl to make cleanup easier on the officer when a suspect urinates, defecates, vomits, or spits all over the back of the car. You'll also find extra blue or red lights on the package deck to help illuminate the patrol unit when running emergency traffic or to keep the officer from being hit from the rear in a traffic stop or traffic-control situation.

The trunk of a patrol unit usually contains a Sterilite box to hold items like crime scene tape; evidence bags; crime scene processing kits; personal protective equipment (PPE) such as rubber boots, Tyvek suits, duct tape, gloves, respirator, gas mask, and so on; chalk for accident and crime scenes; collapsible cones for traffic control; rain gear; dog treats; dog leashes; more paperwork; paper towels; cleaning products; extra engine oil; a fire extinguisher; extra ammo; spare tire and jack; stuffed animals and stickers to distract kids in difficult situations; and even spike strips that can be deployed in the event of a dangerous high-speed pursuit where a suspect vehicle must be disabled and stopped.

Officers get creative in terms of personalizing their work space. Some have hot and cold consoles to store extra water, cold drinks, and their lunch. Some have CD and USB connections in their cars for audio entertainment on long nights, and some even carry portable DVD players to watch movies (this is not recommended, but it has been done). Back in the day, when police cruisers had VHS vaults (video tape recorders) in their trunk to record their dash cam and audio, officers used to pull out their recordable tape and put in a rented movie, watching the playback on their one-inch-by-two-inch monitor overhead. That worked out great, until the officer had a hot code 3 call, requiring them to run lights and sirens, causing the video to automatically start recording. Yep, they recorded over the VHS movie they rented and then had to reimburse the video store around eighty to ninety dollars for the tape they destroyed. Needless to say, that would usually tend to mark the end of watching movies in the car while on duty for that officer.

Some police officers have religious icons fixed to their dashboard or hanging from the rearview mirror, some put stickers that are usually inappropriate on their cages for suspects to read, some keep photos of their families taped to their instrument panel, and some have the police officer's prayer posted.

Again, the patrol car is the officer's home for eight, ten, or twelve hours each day, so it's important to be comfortable, but not too comfortable. Keep in mind, situational awareness is all important, especially when you are driving a billboard that often attracts wanted and unwanted attention.

Just like your patrol car is your office, your "Batman Belt" (duty belt) will become a significant part of your identity and daily life as a police officer. They are generally made of nylon, leather, or patent leather, and can weigh as much as thirty pounds, depending on what you or your agency decides you will have on it.

Of course, there are certain items you will be required to have on your duty belt, including your duty weapon (handgun), at least one pair of handcuffs, a police radio ("portable" for short), and in this day and age, probably a Taser. Optional equipment might include: an extra set of cuffs (chain or hinged), rubber gloves (for use in evidence collection or handling suspects who are bleeding or effusing bodily fluids), perhaps an ASP (collapsible steel baton) or PR-24 (another type of baton or nightstick), a clip for your keys (including handcuff key), a wireless microphone unit for your in-car audio/video recording device, pepper spray, and a pocket knife of some kind. So, you can see how your duty belt could pick up weight, and I think it's pretty obvious why you might need these tools.

Beyond your duty belt, you will be lugging around extra weight in other locations on your body. These items might include: a Kevlar vest (body armor), a body camera, a portable digital pocket recorder, a notepad, at least two pens, reminder cards for drug recognition or Miranda warnings, a backup gun under your shirt in a holster attached to your vest or around your ankle under your pants, another knife clipped under your vest, sunglasses, your lucky St. Michael (the patron saint of police officers) medallion on a neck chain or a coin in your pocket, your wallet or money clip, photos of your family, a watch, your cell phone, a wedding band or ring, a hat (if required), an LED flashlight or MAG light, and a traffic vest when you're involved in traffic control or working an accident on a roadway, and depending on what you are responding to, you may even have a riot shield, riot helmet, riot baton, shotgun, assault rifle, pepper-ball gun, stop sticks, handheld radar unit, motorcycle helmet, rain gear, and so on.

You will actually pursue suspects on foot carrying some if not all of these things, and the suspect/s will be in tennis shoes, in varying states of dress or undress, and citizens will criticize you for letting them get away. Why couldn't you keep up? Why didn't you jump that twelve-foot-high fence after them?

10

GOING TO COURT

Every time you make an arrest, and often when you issue a traffic citation, you can bet you'll receive a subpoena (an order from the court to appear on a specific date at a specific time) to make a court appearance. These court dates, whether they occur on your scheduled day off or work day, will take up a significant amount of your time, sometimes with overtime compensation, but many times without extra pay. Unless you are assigned to day shift, which as a new officer you certainly will not be (that shift is reserved for officers with serious seniority), going to court will either extend your work day at the beginning or end, or fall on your day off and ruin your weekend plans. Just expect it and accept it.

There are a variety of courts you may be subpoenaed to, and in some cases, depending on where they are eventually resolved, it may require more than one appearance in more than one court, barring any continuance (rescheduling of the initial court date). These courts include city court, usually traffic court or the court where minor city ordinance violations are disposed of; general sessions court, the lowest court in the county or parish, usually where misdemeanors are handled or probable cause is determined when a felony has occurred in order to move the case to circuit court; circuit court, where felony charges are handled for offenses against the state; federal court, where federal offenses are prosecuted; civil court, where custody of minor children and property rights are often determined; and finally juvenile court, where offenses involving suspect/s who are under eighteen years of age are handled.

So what does your average court appearance look like? Well, again, it depends on which court you are subpoenaed to appear before. For instance, in traffic court, you'll arrive ten to fifteen minutes before the proceeding and have your overtime slip signed by the clerk, if applicable. Then you'll wait for your case to be called. The city judge will hear the testimony of the defendant, you'll give your testimony as the citing officer, and the city judge will make a decision. Usually, this is in favor of the officer and will involve the defendant paying a fine, court costs, or attending traffic school if the offender has committed a moving violation.

In general sessions, again, you'll arrive early, clear security at the county or parish courthouse, have your overtime slip signed by the assistant district attorney (ADA), and then review the case with the ADA. The ADA will then hear the testimony of the defendant or the defendant's attorney, and an attempt will be made to settle the case, resolve it with a plea bargain, bind it over to the grand jury to see if it will go directly to circuit court, or have a probable cause hearing to determine if there is a justification to move the case to circuit court for disposition.

By the time a case reaches circuit court, either through the grand jury returning a true bill (finding that there is probable cause for the case to move forward into circuit court) or the case having been bound over in general sessions, the defendant will either plead guilty to the original charge/s or to a lesser agreed-upon charge/s, or the case will go to trial and the jury selection process will begin (voir dire). If a case is solid, it is rare that it will go to trial, in my experience. Once a verdict is reached in circuit court, either through a plea or jury trial, the judge will set a date for sentencing and will sentence the convicted individual/s based on a strict set of sentencing guidelines handed down by the state. Federal court works much the same way as circuit court, only the demeanor of the courtroom and attorneys is much more serious and stringent, as are the outcomes.

Juvenile court is a very different animal than any of the courts previously discussed. The first, and most important, difference is that the defendants are all under the age of eighteen, and the purpose of the court is not punitive—to punish or penalize defendants—but to help get them back on the right track (rehabilitate) and offer guidance in the process. The court is a little more informal, and the judges (attorneys) are usually not elected but rather appointed by a sitting judge and referred to as juvenile court referees or justices. They are, for all intents and purposes, there to ensure that the juvenile's rehabilitation is provided for and that the child has an advocate assigned to follow through with the process. Of course, a hearing does take place, and the juvenile may or may not be represented by an attorney. The state is represented by an ADA. Instead of a guilty or not-guilty verdict being handed down from the juvenile court, the defendant will either plead true or not true. Or, if a bench trial is held, the judge will determine a verdict of true or not true after hearing all of the testimony and evidence in the case.

Infrequently, you may be subpoenaed to civil court, usually because a couple in a domestic or divorce suit want to use your testimony to damage their rival for the purpose of winning custody of minor children, property, or money. These court appearances are not fun, and the attorneys usually attempt to distort your testimony to win their client's case. Avoid these when you can, and if you cannot get out of making an appearance, stick to the facts and the facts only, because you may be called to testify for either side, and you really don't want to take a side. If you do, you'll likely be subpoenaed again if the case drags out, which will be a further tax on your time and day/s off.

Know this: regardless of which court you appear in, informal score is kept by your agency. Your reputation as a police officer, and later as an investigator or supervisor, will be partly determined on how many cases you successfully prosecute before the courts. You should keep track of these statistics and cite them when you are up for promotion. It could make the difference between advancing your career in law enforcement and being a patrol officer for twenty-five years. Also, you should begin building solid cases that will hold up in court when you respond to a call or intervene in an incident on the street. What you do at that time, your actions or inaction, will have an impact on whether or not you secure a conviction of the defendant in the court system. So follow your policy, procedures, and state law to the letter. Establish good relationships with the officers of the court, and document everything you observe and do in detail, complete with statements from the victims and defendant/s whenever possible. Nothing convicts like someone's own words in their own handwriting and/or video and audio recordings made at the time of the incident.

Also, make sure you assemble and process all evidence related to the crime and arrest, and take it with you to court. Write a thorough report and take that with you to court; don't trust your memory, it will fade over time. And don't take outcomes personally. You will lose some, in spite of taking all the right steps from start to finish. But don't worry. Chances are, if you work in your jurisdiction long enough, you'll have another chance with the same defendant. In cop parlance, these people are referred to as "frequent flyers" and "regular customers," but more appropriately, you can refer to them as "repeat offenders."

Finally, here's a tip. Don't discuss your court case with defense attorneys prior to taking the stand in the courtroom. They are not your friends, no matter how much they joke with you and talk about the game they watched over the weekend and the goofy people they are representing. I can all but guarantee you that if you clue them in on the particulars of the case prior to taking the stand, you will find that the facts surrounding their client's arrest that you provided will come up in the court room and be used in a way favorable to their client, not the state, which you represent along with the ADA.

Oh, and one more thing. You are still a citizen and may be called to serve on a jury. The way to avoid this is simply to let the clerk who issued the subpoena or attorneys involved in the case in jury selection know that you are an active law enforcement officer. This is usually viewed as a prejudice, and you will likely be excused.

11

VANDALISM, LITTERING, AND OTHER CRIMINAL MISCHIEF

In 1976, one of the southern states aired a popular Public Service Announcement (PSA) on television about not littering, complete with its own theme song written and recorded by a country music star. You can still find the video on YouTube, and the campaign featured a disheveled guy wearing a dirty, greasy tank top throwing trash out of an old, beat-up convertible car onto the highway. Poignant, I know, but effective. If you Google it, I recommend having the word "trash" in your search criteria.

I bring that up to talk about some of the most disgusting crimes that human beings can perpetrate against the property of others, and more tragically, against their own community where they live, work, and re-create every day: vandalism, littering, and other such criminal mischief.

There's nothing worse than being out for a Sunday drive with your family and having to look at trash on the side of the road, litter covering a vacant lot, graffiti on public buildings and signs, broken windows, and other forms of defacement done to real estate that is up for sale and vacant buildings waiting to be occupied. The damage and ugliness affects everyone. It lowers property values, encourages drug users to take over places where people live and turn them into crack houses, makes important road signs unreadable to the motoring public, costs taxpayers money to clean up, and causes insurance rates to climb for business owners and real estate companies alike. Of course, the bottom line is it's just plain unnecessary and nasty.

I can't tell you how many traffic accidents have been caused by missing stop signs at intersections, how many turf wars have been fought between rival gangs over territory they have claimed by marking it with spray paint (tagging), and how many wildfires have been started by cigarette butts thrown out of a moving vehicle by discourteous motorists.

But beyond the obvious, there is something inherently disturbing about the character and mental health of people who would commit these crimes and believe their actions are somehow okay and within societal norms and boundaries of proper behavior. Now before you start thinking I'm Deputy Barney Fife from the popular television program *The Andy Griffith Show*, let me illustrate my point.

I was called one day to the library in our community to take a report from a citizen and the library staff regarding vandalism that had occurred to the bathrooms of the library and to a patron's car in the parking lot. It seems that two teenage males thought that it would be funny to defecate on the floor and then smear it around, collecting some of the waste in a paper towel, hand-carrying it to the parking lot, and dumping it into a vehicle with its window down and a child safety seat in plain view. These guys vandalized those bathrooms and a patron's car that clearly had a small child transported in it with human fecal matter, human waste. It just doesn't get more nasty or disgusting than that. Of course, the teenagers were identified because they were caught on the library's surveillance cameras entering the bathrooms and carrying the waste to the parking lot. They were brought into juvenile court, where not only were they punished and required to make restitution for the damage, but they were court-ordered to undergo mental health evaluations, and child services was assigned to investigate their home environment.

"Okay," you say, "I get the point about littering and vandalism, but what do you mean by criminal mischief?" Well, first of all, there really isn't a specific charge for "criminal mischief"; the term is used to describe various crimes, usually misdemeanors, that aren't particularly nefarious but certainly fall into the category of "up to no good." I might place some of the following offenses into this category: truancy (not showing up for school), curfew violations (being out past a certain time as a juvenile), desecration of a grave site, disorderly conduct, public indecency, public intoxication, joyriding, phone harassment, mailbox tampering, using false identification, trespassing, and possession of tobacco by a minor. This is not a comprehensive list by any means, but you get the idea.

Most of these crimes are just a plain nuisance to law enforcement and the public in general and the majority of the offenders, where the above list is concerned, are juveniles. That said, this is where a lot of career criminals start, and it's important as a police officer to address each and every one of these cases. If you ignore them and write them off as someone having a little innocent fun, I can promise that you'll eventually get a call from a property owner, parent, or concerned citizen and end up addressing them in the end. So it's better to be proactive. You might just prevent a teenager from becoming a criminal as an adult, and you will certainly be providing peace of mind to the citizens you serve, all the while ensuring the maintenance of nice neighborhoods and public facilities in your city or jurisdiction.

One beautiful summer day, I was on patrol in our fair city, riding with the windows down in my car and enjoying a peaceful start to my work day when I was dispatched to a very large, stand-alone retail store, popularly identified and associated with a smiley face. This particular store is in just about every community in America.

It seems, based on the information I had received from dispatch, that an elderly male subject had exposed himself to a disabled woman in the parking lot of the store while performing a certain act. Greeeeeaaatttt, I thought, this is just how I wanted to start my shift. With a description of the suspect and his vehicle, I headed in the direction of the discount superstore.

I didn't have a hard time locating the vehicle, its occupant, or the complainant who was waiting safely inside the store in the loss prevention office. She was shaken up and of course highly offended, as was her husband, who responded to the scene to support his wife.

When I made contact with the suspect and ran his driver's license, checked for warrants, and also had a criminal history run, I wasn't surprised to find out that this wasn't his "first rodeo," a slang term police officers often bat around to say, "This guy has done this before." What was surprising, and somewhat entertaining if you find gallows humor (unpleasant and full of irony) funny, was his cover story.

The suspect told me that he had been mowing the grass that morning and had stopped to take a break from the heat, lying down in the grass in the yard of his home. He stated that following his rest, his wife wanted him to drive her to the store, so he agreed. While she was in the big box store and he was waiting outside in his truck with the windows rolled down watching the ladies go by in their summer apparel, he "got an itch." Believing that it might be a tick, he decided to take his pants and undergarment down in the parking lot and search for the tick in his nether regions, all the while scratching where it itched.

While trying to keep a straight face, I listened to the story, and although I found it entertaining, it didn't really jive with the report I received from the victim concerning the back and forth motions of his hand and its position on a certain body part. Couple that with the suspect's history and the victim's written statement, and suffice it to say I transported the subject to a place where he could continue to cool off on that hot summer day—the location commonly referred to as, "the cooler," "the clink," "the icehouse," and so forth. The county jail.

12

UNWANTED SUBJECTS

When police officers respond to an unwanted subject call, they never know exactly what the situation is going to be until they get there, but it's a pretty good bet that at a bare minimum they are going to have to ask someone to leave the premises who doesn't want to. That, by definition, is the nexus of an unwanted subject call.

Of course, not unlike most calls for service that an officer responds to, it's probably going to be a little more complicated than that.

First, an officer must calm all the parties down if they are overly excited, unruly, or at worst, aggressive. Someone may have to be removed by force or arrested if they are breaking additional laws in the process of refusing to leave, like disorderly conduct (creating an unsafe situation for the officer or other parties involved), public intoxication, or maybe even criminal trespass if they have been warned by a sign that is posted or been given a verbal or written warning on another occasion.

Beyond those considerations, and something of a great deal of importance to the officer in terms of handling the situation, will be whether or not the person has a legal right to be where he or she is. For example, if the person is in public (at a business or restaurant), the manager or owner of the business has a right to refuse service to a patron. However, if the person is refusing to leave a domicile where that person has standing— for example, the person lives there legally because he or she pays rent, is on the lease, or has established residency by receiving mail there—the person cannot be forced to leave by an officer. A civil course of action will be necessary, as well as a legal eviction initiated by the responsible party or landlord.

Officers will typically attempt to earn the unwanted subject's voluntary compliance in exiting the premise if appropriate, but if the situation escalates, force may have to be used. Again, the officer must exercise good judgment and common sense in acting, especially where force is going to be applied. Chances are, regardless of the subject's standing, if force is utilized there will be at a minimum a complaint and possibly a lawsuit if there is a question as to the subject's standing.

While we're on this subject, now might be a good time to talk about when an officer has a legal right to be in a location, conducting an investigation, and when you can tell the officer to leave.

First, if police officers are responding to a call for service—for example, you called them there or someone else did because there is a crime in progress—the police have a right to be there and to investigate until reasonable suspicion is satisfied. This means that the complaint is either determined upon investigation to be unfounded, or probable cause for an arrest or warrant to issue is arrived at. The caller/complainant can ask the police officers to leave if the caller has an interest in the home or building, but you can't make cops leave or just slam the door on them, refuse them entry, or force them out.

That said, the Constitution of the United States protects citizens from exposure to unlawful search and seizure in their home. However, that only applies to an officer entering your home and searching for evidence or seizing your person (effecting an arrest) where there is 1) no lawful reason for them to be there, and 2) no reasonable suspicion or probable cause to believe a crime has been committed, is being committed, or is about to be committed. Also, it does not protect you if you invite them in, call them for help, or give them verbal or written consent to enter or search the premises. Here's an example of an unwanted subject call that transpired in a public place: the community hospital.

For some, Easter is viewed as a holiday set aside to celebrate the risen Savior, his ascension into Heaven, and his promise to return one day to gather his flock unto him. It's certainly not a day to cause or participate in mayhem, and especially not in the hospital chapel where people come to pray for the healing of loved ones and the strength to endure physical pain and suffering. But this was not going to be your ordinary Easter Sunday.

It was 2005, and I was in my third year as a police officer with the new just beginning to rub off, but not enough seniority to escape working on the holiday. It was Saturday night, and by the time I ended my shift at 1 a.m., it would be Easter Sunday. I was halfway through what had been a quiet night and I expected to end it that way, but of course, I had jinxed myself with that expectation.

The silence of my night was broken at 7:45 p.m. by three alert tones and the dispatcher relaying my call number on the police radio. I answered with the same and was subsequently dispatched code 3 (emergency response) to the medical center emergency room where hospital security had corralled a large, male subject, who was reportedly in the process of tearing the ER chapel apart. Yep, not your typical call for service or unwanted subject call.

I arrived at the entrance to the ER where I was met by an admitting nurse who told me that the suspect, Christopher, had been brought in earlier in the day by police officers from our neighboring jurisdiction for a mental health evaluation. The nurse said Christopher had been sitting in the lobby all day waiting for the crisis team to respond to the hospital to conduct his evaluation and determine if he would be admitted to a mental health facility as an inpatient. "It took three police officers to get him into the emergency room," said the nurse. "If I were you, I'd wait for some backup."

I glanced across the busy ER waiting area to see two hospital security guards standing at the entrance to the chapel, and knowing backup was already on the way, I headed in their direction. As I parted the two security officers at the door I got my first look at Christopher. The nurse had not exaggerated, he was definitely a big guy, but his physique was more akin to Humpty Dumpty than a football player.

Everything in the ER chapel was broken and on the floor, from furniture and pictures to flowers and altar vases. In fact, the only piece of furniture that wasn't overturned or broken was the chair Christopher was sitting in at the far end of the chapel. As I walked toward Christopher I couldn't help but notice that his knuckles were white as he tightly grasped the arms of the chair, his face was beet red, and he was breathing heavily as if he had just finished the New York City marathon. Beside Christopher's chair was an open, full bottle of soda that the security officers had given Christopher as a peace offering, hoping to calm him down.

I knew Christopher was not going to respond in a positive manner to force, so I thought I'd buy some time for my backup to arrive by attempting to develop a rapport with Christopher and ease the tension a bit. Addressing Christopher in a nonconfrontational and soothing voice, I inquired as to what the problem was and how I could help him. Christopher said that he "wanted to see a doctor" and that he "had been waiting a very long time!" I reassured Christopher that the hospital staff was working on that issue and he could expect to see a physician very soon. I didn't really believe this would satisfy Christopher, but what the hell, it was worth a shot. Unfortunately, I was right.

Christopher didn't want to be reassured. He wanted to continue his tirade. Reaching for the open bottle of soda beside his chair he grabbed it, stood up, and threw it as hard as he could at the wall on the opposite end of the chapel. The bottle exploded on impact, subsequently sending soda everywhere, including running down the walls of the chapel. Well, that was about enough as far as I was concerned, and it seemed to me that at the moment Christopher needed a jail cell more than the services of the crisis team.

I latched onto Christopher's left arm, spun him around, and snapped the handcuffs on him just as my zone partner entered the chapel. We grabbed Christopher under his arms, because he refused to walk, and dragged him yelling and screaming from the chapel and through the ER waiting area.

My partner and I paused with Christopher between the two automatic breezeway doors and had a little discussion with him concerning his demeanor. Having had that discussion, we exited the breezeway and put Christopher into the back of my patrol car, where he quit screaming in favor of spitting all over the back glass, cage, and windows.

Christopher's brother had just arrived at the ER and was pleading with me not to take him to jail. At the same time my shift sergeant was encouraging me to get Christopher away from the hospital and to the Criminal Justice Center.

I keyed up the mic to my police radio and advised dispatch that I had one in custody. I reported the gender of my suspect and gave the mileage on my patrol car odometer, as required by policy when transporting a member of the opposite sex. Christopher started yelling at the top of his lungs again before I could even get out of the hospital parking lot. Of course, all the officers on our primary channel could hear him in the background of my transmission. One of our K-9 officers, who, coincidentally, was just turning into the ER, asked if I would like him to follow me to the jail. I keyed up my mic again and acknowledged the wisdom of that offer.

Sure enough, we had not gone more than three blocks before we had to stop. Christopher had lain across the back seat of my patrol unit and was trying to kick out the side window. Amazingly, he didn't succeed, but he did manage to dislodge the window from its track, causing it to protrude away from the car at a forty-five degree angle.

After yet another "Come to Jesus" meeting in the parking lot of a local bank, where we threatened to hobble (place one end of a strap around the suspect's ankles and shut the other end in the car door) Christopher's feet if he didn't stop this behavior, he began to calm down. The meeting was appropriately named, as Christopher advised me that he was "the Son of God." Christopher continued to proclaim his divinity between requests for me to roll the back windows down so he could get some air. I just couldn't resist. I replied to Christopher's request by declaring that if Christopher was indeed the "Son of God," he could roll the window down without my assistance.

I arrived at the Sally Port (similar to a garage, but having a roll-up door on both ends) of the jail, knowing that the booking officers would refuse to admit Christopher to the Criminal Justice Center if he was in need of medical attention. So, to ensure that I wouldn't have to return Christopher to the emergency room, where I would have to babysit him all night until he was committed, I sat him on a park bench outside of the jail with several officers.

I secured the mittimus (admitting paperwork) on Christopher and escorted him into the jail and drove away, hoping to clear the Criminal Justice Center before the corrections officers had the opportunity to interact with him!

I had just started eating my dinner from a local fast-food restaurant when the call for service came out over the radio in my patrol car. "2320, 2259 to back, code 2 for an unwanted subject at Marsh's department store, Cold Springs Market/Mallard Lane."

I tossed my food into the passenger floorboard, threw the gearshift into drive, hit my lights and sirens, and sped off in the direction of the call. As I pulled into the parking lot of the large strip-mall complex where the department store was located, a Zippy Burger's employee flagged me down. Zippy is located in the parking area, adjacent to Marsh's department store.

I put two and two together, given the employee's hysterical demeanor, and determined that the unwanted subject from Marsh's must have migrated to the fast-food restaurant. I jumped out of my patrol unit and ran toward the door as the employee screamed that two Hispanic males were holding down the unwanted subject. I entered the restaurant and saw two large men with their knees and full body weight on top of the suspect, who was face down on his stomach in front of the counter.

The suspect was a young white male with shoulder-length hair, around six feet tall and probably weighing about 135 pounds soaking wet. I ordered the two Hispanic males to get off of the suspect. I was afraid that with their full body weight on the kid, he would not be able to breathe and might be suffocating.

I grabbed the suspect by his left wrist and arm and attempted to stand him up. However, the suspect seemed unable to stand and went limp. I let the suspect slide back down to the floor, flipped him onto his stomach, and put his left arm and hand in the small of his back. I knelt over the suspect and reached for my cuffs. As I unsnapped the pouch, the suspect flipped onto his back, became very agitated, and started punching and kicking me, all the time yelling something unintelligible about having to go to the bathroom. I got a good look at the suspect's pupils, which were fixed and dilated like saucers. You couldn't even see the whites of his eyes. This is usually indicative of someone that is under the influence of an illegal substance. We would find out later that the suspect had ingested marijuana (a depressant), hallucinogenic peyote buttons (mescaline), hallucinogenic mushrooms (psilocybin), and Adderall (a stimulant). Oh, and he had also been drinking alcohol (another depressant).

I and the other officers in my department had just been issued, trained, and certified on the X26 Advanced Taser, a less-than-lethal weapon featuring a cartridge with two weighted, fish-hook-like probes and twenty-five foot leads inside, all designed to reach out and provide a fifty-thousand-volt shock to a suspect who is actively resisting arrest. The Taser is designed to provide the shock I just mentioned in a five-second cycle when the trigger is pulled and released, or continuously if the trigger is pulled and held, for as long as the battery life lasts (about two hours). When the trigger is pulled on the Taser with the cartridge attached, the

blast doors of the cartridge are blown away and the probes are deployed with the leads trailing behind, one at a ninety-degree angle and the other at a forty-five-degree down angle. There are also hundreds of confetti-like paper dots that have a number on them that are collected as evidence of the deployment by the officer and placed into evidence with the spent cartridge. Suffice it to say, they scatter everywhere like dust in the wind.

At the time of this incident, the Taser appeared on our agency's Use of Force Continuum (see chapter 16) on the same level as pepper spray and soft-hand control in meeting passive resistance. So with the active aggression I was facing, the use of the Taser was justified.

I unholstered my Taser for the first time in the line of duty, focused the laser sight on the suspect, and ordered him to "Stop resisting and stay down!" Of course, he didn't comply, and I deployed the Taser effectively while at the same time notifying dispatch of deployment, continuing my request for backup. My zone partner arrived and attempted to cuff the suspect, but every time the Taser cycle would end, the suspect would continue to resist, each time taking it to another level. Before we were able to apply handcuffs, the suspect "rode the lightning," figuratively speaking, for five five-second cycles: twenty-five seconds at fifty-thousand volts. Whew. In training, I took a five-second hit and that was enough for me. I can't imagine going for twenty-five seconds, but the suspect wasn't feeling any pain, apparently. The Taser is designed to effect compliance in two different ways, through pain compliance and muscle compliance. So if one doesn't affect the suspect, the other will, and trust me, this product works.

Now, you may be asking yourself, does the Taser cause cardiac arrest or a seizure, or any other malady? The answer is emphatically "no," not unless an extenuating or preexisting condition exists that the officer would have no way of knowing. While the Taser delivers an impressive fifty thousand volts of current, it delivers less than an amp of electricity, which is why it won't cause a heart attack or interrupt a pacemaker. Electricity kills with amps, not volts, so the design of the Taser is really cutting-edge. Of course, if a suspect is hiding a crack rock under their tongue and subsequently chokes on it when actively resisting and being Tased at the same time, what can the officer do? Additionally, if the suspect already has a preexisting heart condition, there could be a problem, but again, how would the officer applying the force know?

We did eventually gain compliance. The suspect didn't have any fight left in him after twenty-five seconds with the Taser. We called for EMS to remove the probes and transport the suspect to the ER to treat him for the overdose and Taser burns (minor first degree burns at the connection sites with the skin). When they injected the suspect with the powerful antioverdose drug Narcan or Naloxone, the suspect's demeanor dramatically changed. All of a sudden he was conscious and coherent, and didn't remember being Tased or a thing he had done while under the influence.

As it turned out, the suspect was a juvenile, seventeen years old, and as such I expected to receive a ration of vitriol from his parents when they arrived at the ER about having Tased him. But I was quite surprised when the parents, who had been fully briefed on what had happened, actually supported my handling of the situation, and thanked me for notifying them and providing them with the details about the incident. They actually felt that the Taser preserved their son's life, eliminating the need for the police to use more force rather than harming him in some way. Of course, I was relieved.

The teen was convicted of all charges in juvenile court and sentenced to a year and a half in a very tough wilderness survival program located in the desert. What's more, he was ordered to complete high school upon his return to our community at age nineteen and to travel back and forth to and from school on the school bus. He was not allowed a driver's license, a pretty humbling experience for a young adult.

And you know, the funny thing was, his father was a career drug and alcohol counselor for at-risk teens.

13

TRAFFIC STOPS, VEHICLE PURSUITS, AND ROAD RAGE

A traffic stop is one of the first enforcement acts a new officer learns to perform. It's arguably one of the easiest proactive (self-initiated—not assigned by dispatch) activities an officer can engage in, and without a doubt the genesis of most citizen complaints against cops. People in general, and people who are violating traffic laws in particular, often hate being told what they did wrong or what to do by anyone, especially an authority figure.

Although traffic enforcement and patrol may be the first activity for a recruit or trainee, it may not necessarily be the most boring or safest. Nothing can be taken for granted in law enforcement, even when it involves everyday traffic stops. That's why officers are trained so rigorously before being cut loose to patrol on their own.

Things are not always what they appear to be. It's your duty and responsibility as a cop to differentiate what is commonly expected from the uncommon reality. You've probably heard the words "routine" and "traffic stop" used together often, but let me dispel that myth. There is no such thing as a "routine traffic stop."

Traffic stops, generally speaking, involve several unknown elements and can therefore veer wildly from routine. You never know for sure who you are stopping, what criminal activity they may have engaged in recently, or what potentially troubling items are in the car you are stopping. Even more interesting is that the driver or occupants may have just taken a drug that could kill them or prompt them to attempt to kill you.

The knee-walking drunk may be the mayor or a fellow police officer. The teen on drugs may be the circuit court judge's son. You just pulled over a potential career-ending landmine. Those types of situations take a delicate balancing act, supreme diplomacy, and an immediate call to your sergeant before taking action.

The unaccompanied driver of the new BMW cruising down the high-occupancy vehicle (HOV) lane at eighty miles per hour during peak traffic times will invariably advise you when you pull him over that you need to be looking for the "real" criminals, order you to issue him a warning, and then file a formal complaint against you after you give in and issue him the warning he asked for. That's why it's always better to issue the citation when a driver is disgruntled and likely to file a complaint. Then the officer can avoid this question from the department's internal investigators: "Officer, if the moving violation was so egregious, why didn't you issue him a citation?"

A young man driving a car that is weaving in and out of traffic like he's in a video game will cuss at you like you're a dog when you issue him a citation for speeding and reckless driving. You'll explain to him very nicely that not only could he get hurt driving so poorly, but he could hurt others as well. He will then go home and tell his mom and dad, who are furious that their insurance on junior will go up. Junior will reaffirm his parents' belief that he is a perfect angel, and swear that the cop gave him the ticket for no reason. When that doesn't get traction, he will tell mommy and daddy that the cop was loud and disrespectful to him, which will send the self-important parents over the edge. The next thing you know, they file a formal complaint against you for being disrespectful and unprofessional when you stopped junior, of course conveniently omitting the fact that they weren't even there and that junior is lying to save himself.

The well-dressed businessman may be an embezzling CEO leaving town for the airport before the audit exposes his actions. The guy with the buzz cut may be a neo-Nazi who hates law enforcement and wants to make his mark for the cause. The guy who looks like a normal Joe may be so deep in debt and depression that he has decided on suicide-by-cop. The mom with three kids in the car driving on the wrong side of the road may be drunk or high. Desperate people do desperate things.

Is the innocent-looking minivan a church van or a rolling meth lab? Is there a gun or knife stashed just out of sight but within easy reach of the driver or passengers? Does the vehicle's trunk hold family suitcases full of beachwear and vacation clothes, or drugs, stolen merchandise, or a body? Is there a can of beer, a bottle of booze, a full red Solo cup, or a bottle of clear moonshine in the vehicle? Is that clear liquid in the plastic bottle really water or the illegal gamma hydroxybutyrate (GHB), commonly referred to as the "date rape or club drug," masquerading as H_2O? Has the vehicle been sabotaged with hypodermic needles or razor blades between the seat cushions to cut or impale you when you search the car? You never know what lurks in dark places.

Is the driver driving on a suspended license? Does a passenger have an outstanding warrant that will send him back to jail if caught with a gun in his possession? Are there illegal immigrants in the vehicle? Is the vehicle stolen? Is the vehicle associated with a crime? Are the individuals in the vehicle fleeing from a crime? These drivers may initially stop and then flee, taking you along for the ride or trying to run you over as they escape. Or they may flee immediately, putting you and citizens at risk. I knew a highway patrol officer who was dragged down the interstate after the driver he had pulled over rolled the window up on the trooper's arm, pinning him to the vehicle, and then took off down the highway with the trooper attached to the side of the vehicle. The driver accelerated to over seventy miles per hour. The trooper was lucky to have survived the traffic stop.

Routine? Not hardly. Add darkness to the equation of a traffic stop, and the odds worsen that something can go wrong. That's why officers are trained to be cautious when approaching an occupied vehicle on a traffic stop, at any time of the day or night.

It all starts with the officer on patrol in their car. Contrary to the myth, most traffic stops are made by officers on the move in traffic, not from officers skulking behind a billboard, lying in wait like a scene from the movies *Smokey and the Bandit* or *Super Troopers*. Usually a traffic stop is initiated by an officer driving down a city street, county road, or maybe the interstate when he or she witnesses a moving violation committed by a motorist. The violation could be speeding, following too closely, failure to wear a safety belt, improper driving in an HOV lane, failure to obey traffic signals, or reckless driving.

Other stops may be due to a vehicle equipment violation such as no tail light or headlight, no license plate displayed or an expired tag, improper securing of a truck's load, loud music or noise emanating from or being made by a vehicle, or even a window tint violation.

As an officer patrols and sees a potential violation, he or she quickly assesses the situation and decides if there is a legal reason for a traffic stop. If there is a violation, the officer sometimes positions the patrol car in traffic behind that of the violator and observes for a moment or two to determine how many occupants are in the vehicle. The officer is determining if there is any strange activity taking place in the vehicle compartment, where the vehicle is from, and who it is registered to by running the vehicle's tag number through dispatch or checking it out on the mobile data terminal (MDT) in the patrol car. Then the officer will look for a safe place to signal the motorist to pull over, call out the traffic stop's location to dispatch, engage their emergency equipment (lights and/or siren), and pull the vehicle over to the shoulder.

Stopping a vehicle for a traffic stop is more complicated than it appears. An improper stopped position for either vehicle could be dangerous for the officer and citizen. Officer safety is the first concern of every officer. An incapacitated officer is unable to help anyone, including fellow officers or citizens.

For that reason, in a traffic stop, the officer offsets the patrol car to the left of the violator's vehicle, once the violator's vehicle has come to a complete stop. This offset provides a safer space between the officer and traffic when the officer is out of the police car.

The officer turns the wheels of the unit to the left to ensure that if the police vehicle is struck from behind by another car or truck it will be propelled to the left, away from the violator's vehicle and the officer who has made the stop. Whether the stop is at night or during the day, the officer engages the wall of light, activating the spotlight and take-down lights. These lights flood the violator's vehicle compartment and blind its occupants so the officer's movements are not exposed until he or she passes in front of the wall of light. If the officer judges that it's safe to pass through the wall of light, he or she will engage their handheld light and direct it onto the driver's side mirror to temporarily blind the violator and to obscure the officer's approach to the driver's-side front-door post. Moving from the patrol unit through the approximately twenty-one feet to the violator's driver's-side door post is the most dangerous time for the officer during the stop.

Once the officer reaches the violator's vehicle, the officer stops at the driver's-side door post, a tactical, officer-safety position. In this position, the driver would have to turn around in the seat and telegraph his or her movement if he or she were going to attempt to exit the vehicle or to harm the officer. The officer will then advise the motorist as to why he or she has been stopped and request the driver's operator's license, vehicle registration, and proof of insurance. A professional officer does not start the interaction with, "Do you know why I pulled you over?" Officers who start off that way mistakenly believe that if the violator correctly articulates the reason for the stop, the person has admitted guilt. That's just idiotic, and asking for the violator to retort with a smartass response. I could expound on those ridiculous and offensive responses from the motorist, but I think I'll just let your imagination run wild.

Okay, back to our traffic stop. As soon as the officer reaches the door post, he or she is already sizing up the driver, observing the driver's motor skills and level of organization, and checking for violations like the failure to carry the required paperwork in the vehicle or the driver's inability to produce a license.

Where the officer goes from there depends on what the officer observes. The officer may develop probable cause, a set of circumstances that would lead a reasonable person to believe a crime has been, is about to be, or is being committed, based upon what is observed. Then the officer may ask the motorist to step out of the vehicle, or the officer may decide to have the motorist remain in the vehicle. This is usually a matter of officer discretion or the officer's training. That being said, it's never a good sign when the violator immediately exits the vehicle without being asked to do so by the officer, especially if the officer has not exited the police unit. In this case, the officer should use the public address system and order the driver back into the vehicle, paying attention to determine if the violator has a weapon in his or her hand or on his or her person. Another option is for the officer to exit the police unit and order the driver back into his or her vehicle without using the public address system. Either way, the driver needs to get back in the car, or be placed at a position of disadvantage, but under no circumstances should the driver be allowed to advance on the officer's position.

The officer may radio for backup at this point to have a second set of eyes to watch the offender or vehicle occupants or to safely take the offender into custody—uneven odds in favor of the officer.

The officer may determine that additional moving violations have been committed or the driver is impaired. Or the officer could find that the driver has a suspended or revoked operator's license, or even no license to operate a motor vehicle. Based upon their observations, the officer will likely return to the police unit, request backup if necessary, use the computer to check the vehicle's registration and the operator's driving history, and possibly run the vehicle's occupants against the National Crime Information Center (NCIC) database to determine if the occupants have any active arrest warrants.

If the violator and/or occupants of the violator's vehicle are clear on warrants, the officer will determine if he or she wishes to issue a citation. In most instances, the determination of whether to issue a citation is at the officer's discretion and is dependent upon several factors, including the severity of the offense, the driver's driving history, and the offender's demeanor.

Vehicle equipment violations such as no muffler or broken taillights are also actionable. If the officer decides to cite the driver, the officer will fill out a citation and fine sheet prior to returning to the violator's vehicle.

Upon returning to the violator's vehicle, the dialogue will go something like this, "Mr. or Ms. Blank, I've issued you a citation for travelling fifteen miles per hour over the posted speed limit. That's sixty miles per hour in a forty-five-mile per-hour zone, and I've set your court date for Thursday, October 5, 2017 at 7:30 a.m. in city court. I'll need your signature by the X below. Signing the citation is not an admission of guilt; it just means that you agree to satisfy the citation by appearing on the court date I have given you or by taking care of the citation in the mail, as the sheet I am going to give you will explain. If you decide to take care of the citation in the mail, you will not have to appear on your court date. Do you have any questions about what I have just explained? No. Okay then, you drive safely now. You're free to go." Do not say, "Have a nice day." That's another comment that will be heard by the driver with disdain. I mean really, if you were just issued a ticket and now have to pay a fine of $125 and court costs on top of that, you are not going to "have a nice day."

Remember, an officer may use his or her discretion to give the motorist a citation or to decide to simply give the motorist a verbal warning. It is always in the best interest of the violator to be courteous to the officer, provide the officer with requested documentation when asked, and to avoid smart-alecky comments or question the officer's judgment and/or right to issue a citation. These confrontations, even when done with superficial politeness, are not likely to benefit the motorist or influence the receiving of a warning instead of a citation.

Here's a sampling of stupid questions and inappropriate remarks directed at officers from the motoring public, those who have violated a traffic law, and sometimes from those who have not committed a violation but feel they need to hurl a comment at the officer anyway from the passenger seat or back seat of the violator's car.

This is by no means a comprehensive list:

1) *Don't you know who I am?* The inference, of course, is that if you knew who this violator was, or his or her importance, you would certainly not issue a citation for fear that this person would complain about you. That, of course, would have an adverse impact on your career and longevity with the police department. Such people may also be hinting that they are somehow above adhering to traffic laws, and how dare you accuse them of committing a violation or even consider writing them a citation.

2) *When was the last time you calibrated your radar gun officer?* Or, *I demand to look at the readout on your radar gun.* The first question is generally posed by some know-it-all who has watched too many episodes of the popular 1970s television series *CHiPs.*

The answer? Radar units are not calibrated by officers, but by maintenance personnel assigned to the police department. Additionally, calibration records must be subpoenaed prior to the violator's court date and are not available otherwise. The officer does not have them. And lastly, the officer uses tuning forks and an internal test to make sure the radar unit is functioning within tolerances and standards set by the manufacturer at the beginning and end of each shift.

The second statement is a sideways insult directed at the officer. The suggestion is that the officer must be lying about the radar readout or the officer would let you see it, or that the violator has some implicit right to look at it. Again, the first scenario is insulting and the second is not required by departmental policy or state law. So an officer's response might be, "No sir, I'm not going to show you my radar unit, because I'm not required to do so by state law. I am offended that you would suggest that I am lying." I'll see you in court, Matlock. Of course, I would leave out that last part.

3) *The light was orange when I passed under it officer, not red.* Okay Seinfeld, the last time I checked the only colors in the traffic signals in this city were red, yellow, and green. I think you may need to visit your eye doctor, or at the very least, come up with a better excuse for why you tried and failed to beat the changing of the light.

4) *Didn't you see my FOP supporter or PBA supporter bumper sticker on the back glass of my car before you decided to pull me over?* Wow. These types of delusional drivers think that because they were misinformed by their drinking buddies that by contributing twenty-five dollars annually to the Fraternal Order of Police or the Police Benevolence Association and putting a sticker on their car that they are no longer subject to traffic laws in this state. Either they are complete idiots or they are suggesting that the officer has such inferior ethics that he or she can be bought for twenty-five dollars. In any case, these motorists are most likely issued the ticket they deserved.

5) *Can't you just give me a warning?* Yes, I could, but I've already decided not to. I'm not using erasable ink and I certainly didn't waste my time filling out all this paperwork to change my mind now. And no, I don't care how many tickets you bought last year to the policeman's ball, who you know, or how much cleavage you show. Press hard when you sign your name by the X, three copies—I need your signature to come through on the carbons of the ticket.

6) *You can't give me a ticket, I pay your salary.* Really. That's news to me, because when I was at the city clerk's office yesterday and I looked at the property tax records, I learned that Mr. Johnson at 305 Main Street was actually the citizen whose property taxes went to paying my salary this year. Will there be anything else, sir?

7) *I'll bet you're just writing me this ticket to fill your quota, right?* No, I don't have a quota, but I am going to write at least thirty citations per shift to ensure that I'm always busy and don't have to take a real call, possibly making it necessary for me to act as a law enforcement officer, take a report, or even worse, end up in General Sessions court on my day off, since you asked.

Violators who have a clean driving record and receive a citation would be smart to attend traffic court. If they freely and openly admit their guilt and throw themselves on the mercy of the court, they'll probably get four hours of traffic school on the weekend, pay a small court cost, and have the violation expunged from their driving history when they successfully complete the four-hour school. However, if they've offered any of the commentary listed above or made similar statements, they should probably just pay the fine and move on. I can't speak for every officer, but I documented on the citation, for the judge to see, if the violator was belligerent and I usually included specifics. Trust me, an officer will appear on the violator's court date if the violator treated the officer like a jerk. And more often than not, the judge will look at the officer's notations on the citation and admonish the violator accordingly, if he or she doesn't decide to read the violator's statements to the officer out loud for everyone in the court room to hear, confirming that the violator is not only a bad driver but an idiot to boot. Disrespect for the law and people representing the law are not tolerated in court.

If you grew up in the late 1970s or early 1980s, chances are you probably watched and were a fan of a popular movie with a law enforcement character that made the statement "I'm in hot pursuit" every time he chased the bandit. It was also a popular phrase uttered by a character in a television show who was supposed to be representative of a rural sheriff in the southern United States, chasing a couple of brothers engaged in running moonshine in an orange car with a big number on the side and a big flag on the roof. I think you can read between the lines here. Wink, wink, nudge, nudge.

Suffice it to say that those characters and their statements were funny and entertaining, but have little or no correlation with the policies, laws, or dangerous realities of an actual police pursuit of a vehicle or vehicles.

In the first place, police officers are not communicating with each other or dispatch on a citizens' band (CB) radio, nor do they engage in pursuing a suspect in a vehicle before first considering whether or not the fleeing subject and the incident are aligned with their department's policies and their state law governing vehicle pursuits by law enforcement.

Where I worked and in many police departments in the twenty-first century, our pursuit policy was very limited. We could only pursue a suspect in a vehicle if the person had committed or was in the process of committing a violent felony—a pretty narrow window, folks. If you had not committed a homicide, an aggravated assault, an aggravated robbery, a vehicular assault, an aggravated kidnapping, or some other similar act of violence against a person or persons, we were not going to and were not authorized to chase you.

And what's more, even if the above criteria were met, we still had a responsibility to consider road conditions, traffic, the weather, the speed of the suspect's vehicle and our vehicles, and so on when deciding whether or not to engage in a pursuit or disengage from an active pursuit. Additionally, we were constantly advising a supervisor on the radio of current and changing conditions in the pursuit and we were often called off (directed to terminate the pursuit) by that supervisor.

Again, not all agencies have this policy, but most have a similar policy or more restrictive one, and if they don't, just wait for the first fatality to occur as a result of an ill-advised pursuit and once they've settled the lawsuit with the family of the victim/s, they will adopt a new and restrictive pursuit policy. Gone are the days of the buffoonery we discussed at the outset of this section.

So, what really happens during a police pursuit and how is it justified? Well, buckle up and hang on, because I'm about to give you a front seat to the action.

When I was assigned to our department's Flex Unit and we patrolled in unmarked cars and wore street clothes, we were given the responsibility every year at Christmas time of patrolling the large shopping mall in our community, arresting shoplifters, and dealing with other nefarious goings-on at holiday time.

One of the MOs, or modus operandi (methods of operation), that seasoned shoplifters employ is to drive up to the front of a store where merchandise is displayed on a rack near the entry, and have the driver stand by with the engine running. Then, an accomplice darts into the store, grabs as much merchandise as he or she can carry, sprints back to the car, and the car takes off for the nearest clear avenue of escape, which is usually an interstate. We had ten miles of interstate in my jurisdiction, so there was a lot of opportunity for this type of crime.

With that in mind, we were always circling and looking for vehicles that were parked in the fire lanes near entrances to anchor stores at the mall. The fire lane violation was an opportunity to approach and question anyone sitting in a car in these positions, and an opportunity to prevent or catch shoplifters engaging in this activity. If the driver was innocent and waiting to pick someone up who was exiting the store or someone who was disabled, then we didn't give them any grief. We just asked them in the first case to park in a parking space, or if the person was disabled, we didn't do anything.

On the other hand, if we were able to establish reasonable suspicion or probable cause that the person had been or was actively shoplifting, we addressed it in accordance with departmental policy and applicable state laws regarding the offense and warrantless search and seizure.

One day, while I was patrolling in my unmarked unit at the mall, I spotted a vehicle peeling away at a high rate of speed and barking its tires. It was coming from the entrance to one of the mall's anchor stores. I didn't know it at the time, but the people in the car were being pursued by a loss prevention employee of the store and had just shoplifted merchandise. Dispatch would update me with that information over the radio just as soon as the store called in and during my attempt to stop the suspect/s. I initially attempted to stop the vehicle because of the way the driver was handling his car in a densely crowded area. It was reckless, dangerous, and uncalled for under any circumstance.

Officers don't usually stop motor vehicles in parking lots because they are considered private property, but if the occupants are engaged in committing another criminal offense or act that endangers the general public, they might. That being said, I initially followed the vehicle onto the road that runs around the perimeter of the mall, called out the tag and vehicle description over the radio, turned on my emergency equipment (lights) and yelped my siren, indicating that they were to pull their vehicle over to a safe location.

Instead of responding in accordance with our state laws governing the operation of a motor vehicle, when an officer signals the driver to pull over, the suspects ignored me and sped up instead. They ran through a stop sign at a dangerous intersection and rode up on the curb to get away from me. At that point, I activated my full emergency equipment and called for marked police units to respond, in the event that the suspect/s weren't sure if I was the police, though I don't know how this could have been possible. Still, we always give them the benefit of the doubt. Plus, an unmarked unit can only be the lead vehicle in a pursuit until marked units arrive to take its place. A pursuit is much safer when highly visible units are leading the charge.

Now, I didn't know it at the time, but an off-duty state trooper (highway patrol officer) was at the intersection on his way to the mall to Christmas shop when the suspect barreled through the stop sign and over the curb, pursued by an unmarked police vehicle. I'll stop here for just a moment and answer another question that is probably on your mind. Had the suspect committed a violent felony at this point? The answer is yes and no. When you actively run from the police in a motor vehicle, you are engaging in felony evasion and while that is a felony, it's not necessarily a violent felony. On the other hand, if you run over a pedestrian or strike another vehicle in the process, then it becomes a violent felony because your vehicle is considered a weapon being used in the commission of a crime or crimes. Now back to our story.

The off-duty trooper, thinking that something major had happened to cause an officer in an unmarked car to engage in a vehicle pursuit, followed me to provide assistance as he was carrying his off-duty weapon. As luck would have it, the suspect/s turned into a parking area and stopped in a parking stall. We thought they were going to give up at that point, but when we exited our vehicles to conduct a felony stop, the driver of the suspect vehicle threw the car into reverse and attempted to run over the state trooper and me, and then headed into heavy holiday traffic at a high rate of speed toward the interstate.

I won't go into all of the details here, but it's enough to tell you that they led our agency, and two more adjoining agencies, on a high-speed pursuit across three jurisdictions trying to get away. They eventually drove into a dead end and bailed from their vehicle where they were pursued on foot by officers and eventually taken into custody. They were armed with a handgun, had been shoplifting at several stores, and were in possession of drugs and paraphernalia.

Dangerous? Check! Congested traffic? Check! High rates of speed? Check, over one hundred miles per hour on the interstate and eighty miles per hour on city streets at Christmas time! Violent felony? Check! Armed and dangerous? Check! Arrested without incident and convicted of all charges? Check!

So, I'm sure it's pretty clear from my example why law enforcement doesn't elect to pursue a suspect in a vehicle very often and why it is so dangerous to the public and the officers involved. Pursuit is just unnecessary in circumstances where only minor offenses have occurred and lives are not at stake. But keep in mind that these situations are fluid and change quickly, so what starts out as a simple traffic stop for reckless driving can escalate into a full-blown felony pursuit in seconds. Also, I can tell you from experience that every time I have engaged in one of these situations, it scared the hell out of me and it was a white-knuckle adventure that was not fun at all. There are so many less-than-desirable consequences that can and do result from vehicle pursuits and those liabilities are running through every officer's mind when these incidents arise. Still want to do this job? Read on.

These days, people seem to be affected by stressors that just weren't an issue in the mid-twentieth century, mainly because they did not exist. Technology has changed the way we live and communicate, some would say overcommunicate, and there are certainly more mobile options to facilitate that communication, like smartphones, tablets, GPS devices, and in-car entertainment systems including DVD players. People are more distracted than ever behind the wheel. Perhaps that is one reason road rage is more prevalent and drivers are angrier and apt to act on their anger.

Often, road rage occurs when a driver is cut off in traffic by another motorist, or held up due to inattentive driving, or perhaps cannot even maintain their lane, creating a dangerous situation on the roadway and causing other drivers to have to take evasive action. Usually, this results in the offended motorist banging on the steering wheel or dashboard in frustration, honking the horn repeatedly, or rolling down the window and exchanging a few choice words with the violator. Even obscene hand gestures have been known to fly. But where things really get out of hand and require police intervention is when angry motorists use their vehicles as weapons, or produce a handgun to shoot at the alleged violator from their vehicles, or even exit their vehicle in an attempt to assault the other driver or occupants.

When I was on patrol, I responded to a number of these incidents, and I can guarantee as a new police officer, you will too. It may not happen on your first day on the street, or even the first month you're on duty, but it will happen. It's not a question of "if." It's just a question of "when." Let me illustrate the point.

On an average Friday afternoon, when I was assigned to evening shift, 3 p.m. to 1 a.m., I was patrolling the busy corporate/retail area of our city at rush hour near the interstate. It was about five o'clock in the afternoon; you know, when many people are getting off work and the commuters are starting to clog the main arteries of the city.

We had one intersection that was heavily trafficked every day, without exception, in this area. To give you an idea of its size, it was five lanes wide in each direction, for a total of ten lanes, and was controlled by traffic signals that were either timed or activated by pressure plates under the pavement.

I was dispatched to this intersection in response to a road rage incident, where both parties had exited their vehicle and were fighting in the middle of the intersection. When I arrived, traffic was at a standstill and backed up in all directions at the absolute worst time of the day. Would you call this a hazard or dangerous situation? I would, as it increased the likelihood of a motor vehicle accident, impeded other motorists on the roadway, and also created a situation where the angry motorists might be struck by another vehicle or where I might be struck by another vehicle while attempting to break them up and clear the intersection to get traffic moving. I'll explain why articulating how the incident created a hazard was important in just a minute. First, let's run down the facts, no pun intended.

Prior to being dispatched, one of the motorists involved in this incident had cut off the other when entering a turn out lane. The offended motorist was so angry at this rude behavior, that when the alleged offender stopped for the yield sign at the end of the lane, the upset driver who had been cut off exited his vehicle, approached the driver who cut him off, pulled him out of his vehicle, and began striking him in the face. All of this happened while their wives sat stunned in their respective vehicles. The teed off driver pulled the other guy out so forcefully by his shirt that all of the buttons popped off and were scattered across the intersection.

After I broke up the fight and had them pull into a bank parking lot where it was safer to communicate, we got down to the bottom of the situation. Both guys were old enough to be my father, and I admonished them for their immature and frankly ridiculous behavior. Neither wanted to press charges on the other for assault, so I let that go, but I was determined to bring them before the court so the judge could humiliate them in public and perhaps deter them from a repeat incident. So I cited them both into general sessions court on disorderly conduct. One of the elements of disorderly conduct that must be satisfied is the creation of a "dangerous or hazardous situation to yourself or others," so that's why articulating how that situation occurred was so important.

While we are on the subject of "articulation," know that what you write in your report or on your citation is very important and can make the difference between successful prosecutions or no conviction at all. First, you need to know what to write, and second, how to write it. You should always indicate how the facts of the incident meet the elements of the offense you are citing someone for or charging someone with. Also, you need to be detailed, and at the same time know what "not" to write. Your FTO will help you master the art form of report writing. You don't have to be Ernest Hemingway or Virginia Woolf to be effective, but you do have to be thorough and, of course, please proofread your work and utilize spellcheck or a dictionary before submitting your report or citation for review and approval by your supervisor and the court.

Road rage. Yep, it's a real problem in this country, and people are being injured and killed as a result. Here's another reason to take a "chill pill" if you find yourself becoming angry behind the wheel. Today, in a political climate where there are many gun-toting, concealed/open-carry-handgun-permit-wielding gun association members, someone might just shoot you because they feel threatened, they're scared for their family, or maybe they're just plain crazy. Don't believe me? Just turn on the five o'clock news in your community.

I investigated a case of road rage that occurred in a parking lot, of all places. The angry motorist was offended by a lady who accidentally drove down a parking lane the wrong way, or in other words, against traffic. She was so upset by this innocent mistake that she beat on the alleged offender's car and when the mistaken motorist rolled down her window, the outraged woman grabbed her by the neck and starting shaking her and cussing at her, all in front of the wrong-way driver's child. Later, after the aggressor was arrested for assault, she went on the local news and attempted to justify her behavior, stating she would apologize to the wrong-way driver "when the gates of the devil's place frost over!" Okay, she didn't get the cliché right, but you know what she meant. She was convicted of assault, placed on probation for six months, and ordered to attend anger management classes. Hopefully, she learned her lesson, but I have my doubts. Believe it or not, she even had members of her community, through social media, support her bad behavior and applaud her actions, all while verbally bashing the wrong-way driver.

14

CALLS FOR SERVICE

When You Are Called to Serve and Protect

One of the primary responsibilities of patrol officers is answering calls for service. These calls run the gamut from the mundane to the adrenaline-pumping. You might be called to take a report, respond to a crime in progress, or anything in between. Calls are generally assigned to officers via police radio and then alternatively over the Mobile Data Terminal (MDT), if the agency is lucky enough to be equipped in this manner.

When an officer starts their shift, they never know what they'll be doing over the next eight, ten, or twelve hours. That's why officers experience extreme bumps of adrenaline and cortisol several times a day, and many eventually suffer physical damage to their bodies and minds as a result, such as PTSD.

Radio calls generally come out in a few ways. They always start with a dispatcher who takes the initial call from a complainant, quickly categorizes it, summarizes it, and gives it to the officers over the radio as succinctly as possible. Most agencies have their patrol units equipped with Global Positioning Satellite (GPS) capability that enables the dispatchers to recognize and dispatch the units that are closest and available to the call. This cuts the response time, which improves officer safety and contributes to a successful conclusion of the situation.

Calls are generally dispatched and prioritized as one of three types and the officer acts accordingly:

1) **Nonemergency response**. The officer drives within the posted speed limit, obeying all traffic laws. Basically, you get there when you get there.

2) **Nonemergency or possible emergency response,** code 2, as determined by the officer and shift supervisor. This means that the officer, depending on the situation, how far he or she is from the call, and traffic conditions at the time, may elect to respond with lights and sirens.

On a code 2 call, the officer may only drive up to fifteen miles per hour over the posted speed limit and may disregard traffic signals, but only after stopping and clearing each intersection along the way.

3) **Emergency response**. An emergency response or priority call is preceded by three alert tones on the radio, clearing the radio traffic off the air and indicating to all officers that an emergency call is about to be given out. Officers assigned to the call will respond code 3, meaning with all emergency equipment activated. Officers responding code 3 may drive as fast as necessary to arrive at the call safely and may disregard all traffic laws while on the way to the call in order to expedite their response.

Keep in mind that while officers are responding to the call, they are receiving updates via police radio; operating their emergency equipment; negotiating traffic; communicating with other responding officers, supervisors, and dispatchers; and reading updates and directions on their MDT. It's a lot to manage and officers are counting on the general public to respond appropriately to their emergency equipment.

Motorists should pull to the shoulder of the roadway, usually to the right, and come to a complete stop, yielding the roadway to emergency vehicles. Often motorists are distracted by radios and cell phones when driving and do not yield to the officers. Other times, they yield in the wrong direction, impeding the officers' lane of travel. You never know how a citizen will respond to an emergency vehicle, so you need to be cautious when you are closing in on them during a code 3 response.

Failing to yield to an emergency vehicle is against the law and a moving violation. Unfortunately, the reality is that there is usually not an available officer nearby to cite the violating motorist, or the violating motorist is involved in an accident with a responding officer, which is terrible either way. Fortunately, many law enforcement agencies at the local and state level have started campaigns related to "move over" laws recently passed by their state legislatures. These awareness campaigns have gone a long way toward informing motorists as to proper procedures when emergency vehicles approach them on the roadway or are sitting on the shoulder of the roadway during a traffic stop, enforcement action, or call for service.

Officers are taught to always attempt to overtake motorists when running emergency traffic, on the left if possible, which often necessitates that the officer run on the wrong side of the road, against oncoming traffic. An officer will only pass on the right when there is no other avenue of travel, as this is extremely dangerous to the motoring public and the officer. If a motorist hears sirens behind them and yields to the right, as the drivers' manual instructs, and the officer goes right to pass, well, you know what's going to happen, and it's not good.

The officer who doesn't make it to the call is of no use. This is something trainees have a hard time getting into their noggins early in their careers. After all, who doesn't like to drive fast, disobey traffic laws legally, and see their blue lights bouncing off of buildings in the night, in anticipation of getting to fight someone? Of course, this is a dangerous mentality and a difficult one to eliminate in a new officer. There is no substitute for experience, and you hope the recruit gets that experience without being involved in an injury accident that could be a career-ender before they even get started.

As an FTO, I made a habit of encouraging recruits to always be thinking and considering what actions, if any, they should take in a given situation and the possible outcomes of each decision they made. Situational awareness is also important to an officer. I tried to ingrain this in recruits as well. It has to almost be a second sense, so when trouble breaks out in front of them, they already know where they are, can call out their location, and address the situation quickly.

One of the things I always liked to do with trainees and probationary officers was to surprise them during a shift, just out of the blue, asking them to pull over to the shoulder of the roadway. "Where are we?" I would ask. Usually, after the startled trainees pulled themselves back together, reality would set in. You could almost see the gears turning and smoking inside of their heads. I would ask again, "Where are we? I've just been shot and you have to call for backup and EMS (Emergency Medical Service). Hurry up!" I would exclaim. "I'm bleeding out here in the front seat of the patrol car, and you're taking fire from some deranged gunman! Where are we?"

Inevitably, the first time I introduce this exercise to a trainee, the trainee doesn't know where we are. So I sound the buzzer, indicating that I am now dead and challenge the trainee to use what is around us. "Look for landmarks, addresses on businesses, think about the last significant building or land feature you passed." I also instruct trainees to always look at street signs at every intersection they pass through, so they are aware of their location at all times. Eventually, trainees start putting these techniques into practice and by the end of their training phase with me, they always knew where we were when asked.

Orientation is very important to responding quickly and efficiently, using the most direct route to calls for service. Even those of us who were experienced sometimes found ourselves talking out loud and swearing in the car, "Where is this place? Oh crap, I just passed it!" There's nothing more embarrassing for a veteran officer than being the closest unit to a call and the last one to arrive. You either knew where you were going and slow-walked your way there to avoid taking a report or having to roll around on the ground with a suspect, or alternatively, you just flat didn't know where you were. Either way, it's unacceptable for a veteran officer, and your shift partners notice these things. Cops are like elephants. They don't forget.

Always keep this in mind, too, when responding to calls for service: if a citizen lives near the location of the call and has small children, you're bound to be complained about for driving too fast or too erratically to the call. Conversely, if you slow down to allow for this on the way to the call, you'll inevitably draw a complaint from the victim for taking too long to get there. Yep, you can get gigged for just doing your job when you're a police officer. It's one of the perks no one tells you about. Eventually you find out the hard way.

Back to the topic at hand, calls for service. Once you arrive on scene at any call, the first thing an officer has to determine is what's going on and "which one of these kids is doing their own thing," much like the skit on the popular public television program *Sesame Street*. An officer needs to be observant and look for someone behaving in a way that is not normal or be looking for something in the situation that is out of place or doesn't belong there. If it's a nonemergency call with only a victim present, it's usually pretty easy, if the victim has a few brain cells to rub together and isn't overly dramatic or emotional.

Still, the officer must listen critically to what the victim says to determine if a crime has been committed, where the crime was committed, when it was committed, who was involved, and with what sort of weapon. You know, the basic who, what, when, where, and how. If you're really interested you might even ask why, but motive is a dangerous road to go down with a victim, as it consumes an inordinate amount of time out of service on the call. You usually end up knowing more that you want to know and spending way too much time on scene listening to the victim when you could be knocking out your report and getting back on the street to answer more calls.

Police officers and their respective supervisors are more interested in quantity, the basic facts, and manpower issues. Quality is a nice bonus, when possible. However, it's not the most important issue, just as motive is not important. In patrol, we generally leave the "why" questions to the detectives. If you spend too much time as a patrol officer with the question of why, you'll be getting visits from your supervisor on scene explaining to you that you have been out here on this report call for forty-five minutes while your zone partner has been running call to call. He will tell you to get what you need, wrap it up, and get back out there in service. Oh, and by the way, he'll say, they're testing for detective in a few weeks, so you might want to put in your letter of interest, since you like investigative work so much. Sarcasm is a cop's second language, and they are fluent.

On a take-a-report call, it may not be necessary to take a report. Since time is of the essence, knowing when to take a report and how to avoid taking a report is an art form and definitely one practiced by many, if not most, officers on a regular basis. One of the first questions an officer should ask on a report call is, "When did this incident occur and where?" If the incident occurred in another jurisdiction, no report is taken. If it's a motor vehicle accident report and the wreck occurred on private property or is delayed in being reported, no report is taken. If the incident is civil in nature, no report is taken. If the report involves the seeking of a warrant against another person who has already had you thrown in jail—for example, a grudge report—no report is taken. If the victim is intoxicated and the crime is not against a person, no report is taken.

Beyond those obvious "no report" situations, the officer listens critically to what is being said and will attempt to avoid taking the report if the incident can be handled in any acceptable, alternative way. Barring that, the officer takes a report. Sometimes, it takes longer to convince the victim that they do not need a report than it does to just take the report. This takes experience and is often a "finesse thing."

To be sure that you get to take a report, make sure you are the first to arrive on scene. So, conversely, another way officers avoid taking a report is to arrive last on scene. It is generally accepted that the first officer to arrive on scene and to take control of the situation takes the offense report and makes an arrest if necessary or issues citations. So if you don't like taking reports, it pays to take your time getting there with regard to most calls for service.

If you arrive at a call after an emergency response, you should just plan on the situation or scene being messed up. Someone's teeth will be lying on the floor; someone will be falling down drunk; someone will be holding a gun to their head; someone will have sawed their lover's couch in half with a chainsaw or bashed the hell out of their new Porsche; or maybe someone's father or mother never returned with the kid after their court-appointed visitation. And, if you're really lucky, you've already responded to this call twice tonight and seven times this week. You'll know all the players.

But don't feel like you're the Lone Ranger in a difficult situation. When an officer cannot resolve a situation, you just call for a supervisor. Supervisors theoretically have more experience and may know someone or something you don't, in which case, it's a learning opportunity for the officers who responded initially. Or, you, the officer, already know what needs to be done, but you want the supervisor to make the decision, so if something goes south, you're off the hook.

Just be careful with corralling your supervisor to step into the mess. Do it too many times and the supervisor, who is usually more experienced than you in all the tricks of the trade, will paint you into a corner that you cannot get out of without a write-up or, at the very least, a headache.

Finally, if you respond to a call, let's say a felony incident where evidence is available to process, you'll need to have your supervisor call the Criminal Investigation Division (CID) on-call supervisor to see if a detective is going to respond. Generally, you can count on the on-call detective not responding, unless it's a homicide or a burglary to the home of a prominent member of the community.

And lucky you, you'll have to explain their lack of response to the victim without throwing CID under the bus and creating a lack of confidence by the public and simultaneously pissing off CID. You want to, but bite your lip so you don't tell the victim, "It's Sunday, the football game is on, and your unfortunate incident just isn't important to CID. However, a detective might (emphasis on "might") call you on Monday, but I can't guarantee that." The best you'll be able to do is apologize to the victim profusely and indicate that a call from a detective may come at the beginning of the coming week, but that when and if they receive a call will depend on the case load of the assigned detective. You'll give them the number to CID so they can pester the heck out of them, and they'll leave you alone to go back to your patrol duties.

15

DOMESTIC DISTURBANCES

Dangerous and Unpredictable

One of the most dangerous calls you'll ever respond to as a police officer is a domestic disturbance. Sounds like a husband knocked over the wife's garden gnome, doesn't it?

"Disturbance" not hardly! The term "domestic disturbance" makes the hair stand up on the back of my neck just thinking about it. When the call comes out, you'd better get on your game. The reason it is so dangerous is simple: you have no idea what you're getting into.

You may be responding to an ear-splitting verbal squabble that will trash every lamp and dish in the house but not harm a single hair on a person's head, or a fight-to-the-death cage match complete with artillery.

While you're squealing up to the house, you run the scenarios through your mind. Your adrenaline starts coursing through your veins. But, whatever you do, don't park your patrol unit right in front of the house. Park in front of the next-door neighbor's residence and proceed the rest of the way on foot when your backup arrives on scene. I cannot tell you how many officers have been shot in or getting out of their patrol units by an angry, armed suspect lying in wait for the police after ending the life of a victim. All right, back to the questions you should be asking yourself.

Are the opponents armed? Are they fighting in the kitchen or garage where there are a dozen deadly weapons within arm's reach?

Are they sober as saints or drunk as skunks? Are they riding high on PCP or ketamine, making them as strong as silverback gorillas with just about as much respect for the law as gorillas?

Are they duking it out alone, or is there potential for it to turn into a tag team match with friends and family who have gathered for the show? Are there kids who are terrified and hiding or trying to defend someone? Is the family dog wigged out and biting everything and everyone that moves?

Are the injuries just bruises and scratches, or is someone spewing blood like a sprung garden hose? Are there teeth on the floor?

Is someone being chased around the yard by a loved one in a two-ton pickup truck?

Is all hell breaking loose inside the house, and no one will call a timeout long enough to open the door for you?

Even scarier, is it all quiet when you arrive? Is someone inside dead? Is there a hostage situation? Does the strung-out girlfriend-murderer have you in the crosshairs of his high-powered hunting rifle from the upstairs window? Has the aggressor left the home and hidden outside with an assault rifle, waiting for you to get into range?

Most of the time you don't know what is going on between two or more people who live under the same roof. You don't know how the parties involved are related or how long the incident has been building up or going on. You also don't know how emotionally involved the parties are—way too many unknowns for any officer to be comfortable with. An officer who gets comfortable on a domestic call is likely to wind up being a statistic on the National Law Enforcement Officers' Memorial in Washington, D.C.

So, you're pumped up on high-octane adrenaline and headed in a red-hot heat with lights and sirens to a domestic. You arrive on scene and wait. Yes, wait. One of the first things for any new officer responding to a domestic disturbance call to remember is: wait for your backup to arrive before making contact, unless you are sure that someone's very life is in imminent danger. Four eyes are better than two in volatile situations. When two officers enter a domestic-disturbance call, parties can usually be separated safely and the officers can watch each other's back effectively. Where two or more officers are present, chances are that it will take less force to resolve the incident if the parties are still engaged in violent behavior when officers arrive on scene.

Take, for instance, the time an officer responded to a domestic disturbance call and entered the scene before his backup arrived. While time is certainly of the essence, it doesn't mean ignore your training and common sense. The officer catapulted out of his patrol car and sprinted to the door. In plain view through the open door was a male subject who was on top of a female, beating her to a pulp. The officer happened to be a smaller officer who could not physically remove the male subject and restrain him from committing further violence against the female subject. As a result, the officer, who was alone and had already made entry, had to light up the male subject with his Taser to gain compliance and to get him off of the female he was beating up.

Had the officer waited for a backup unit to arrive, the need to use a Taser would have likely been eliminated, and the two officers would have been able to physically get the male subject under control. The male subject would have realized he was outnumbered and outgunned, and climbed off of the female subject when ordered to by the officer on scene. This would have allowed them to safely control and resolve the situation.

There are also times when even two officers aren't enough on a domestic disturbance call. It's not unusual for two people who are related and involved in a violent confrontation to stop fighting each other and to turn on responding officers in an "us-versus-them" mentality. These are the kind of incidents when a suspect jumps on the officer who is trying to contain another party to the conflict. When this general craziness erupts, it is usually fueled by alcohol, drugs, or both. Let's face it, if you decide to fight with the cops you may win the fight, but you are going to lose the battle in the end. You have to be crazy or under the influence of an intoxicating substance to fight with the police. Rational, sane, sober people do not engage in fighting police officers.

Upon gaining safe, legal entry into the house and prying any fighting folks apart, you usually quickly hear loud and clear what the combatants think about your presence, your profession, your personal appearance, your intelligence, and often your family. If they are referring to you by colorful names, it may not be easy to cajole them into voluntarily accompanying you to the patrol car and to jail.

You may have to consider more, uh, *persuasive* ways to convince that person to comply with your goal. This is where your training comes in, but just as important, your instincts to anticipate when someone is about to do something stupid, like take a swing at you or to shout to their adult son in the back of the house to come out and "shoot the pigs!" Either way, be on your toes. Hope for the best and plan for the absolute, most bizarre worst.

It's the odd situation that you have to worry about, and you never know when it's going to come down the pike, so you had better be prepared for the unexpected, always. Wait on your backup, separate the parties, watch each other's back, and take the primary aggressor (the one most responsible for the violence) to jail.

If the judicial system does its job, that will ensure peace between the combatants, at least for the next few hours until they're released with bond conditions that hopefully enjoin the offender from coming around the victim, possessing a weapon, or engaging in threatening the victim in any way. Violate those conditions, and it's back to jail for the offender with no bond.

Keep in mind that restraining orders and civil process only fine offenders if they violate the conditions of the order. While orders of protection or bond conditions have more teeth, they are still no guarantee that an offender will not locate the victim while free on bond and finish the job he or she started. I mean seriously injure or kill the victim. It's really incumbent on the responding officers, the magistrate or judicial commissioner, and the judge to know the history of the offender and, where previous violence exists, deny bond to ensure the victim remains safe. Keep the offender locked up so the violent offender cannot offend again, at least for a good, long while. That's the idea and the best-case outcome.

If you don't believe that, then consider this. A suspect who was arrested on a domestic violence charge and was being held without bond due to his violent history came before a general sessions court judge in our jurisdiction. The judge, in his infinite wisdom, decided to grant the offender bond instead of holding him without bond until he was convicted in circuit court and sentenced to prison.

Even though the judge issued an Order of Protection and set bond conditions on the offender, the first thing the accused did upon release, pending his next court appearance, was to return to the home of the victim, his fiancé, and finish the job he previously started. Only this time, he used a claw hammer. Not only did he beat his fiancé to death in the driveway of her home, he almost killed her grandmother too, and would have had the decedent's grandfather not showed up with a shotgun and ran the suspect off at gunpoint.

It was a beautiful Saturday in July of 2004, my second year on the job, and I was assigned to the 3 p.m. to 1 a.m. shift. We had just finished roll call and I was about to leave the station when I received a "speak-to-officer" call from dispatch.

Speak-to-officer calls can be about anything, and usually amount to nothing. They can involve everything from a resident concerned about children playing in the street to noise complaints, from suspicious persons observed by the neighborhood watch to property-line disputes. You never really know what you are going to encounter until you arrive on scene.

As I made my way from the station to the complainant's address, I read a short narrative on my MDT about the call. Apparently, the complainant, Hope, was separated from her husband, Joe, after he had assaulted her in their home situated in the city adjacent to ours. Hope wanted to speak with me regarding financial papers that Joe had allegedly removed from her new residence in our city.

I made contact with Hope at her new home in a nice, suburban neighborhood. Hope told me about the encounter with Joe that led to his arrest on domestic violence charges and his subsequent bond conditions that instructed Joe not to have any verbal, electronic, or in-person contact with Hope. Hope showed me a copy of the paperwork. Sound familiar?

Hope went on to tell me that since the bond conditions were issued, Joe had called her on the telephone repeatedly and finally showed up at her new home one afternoon, a few days before she called me.

Hope said that when Joe showed up, he blocked her car in the driveway, got out of his car, and grabbed her by the arm, forcing her to sit down on the porch and listen to him as he attempted to talk her into dropping the domestic violence charges against him and ending the divorce proceedings Hope had initiated.

Hope told me that when she refused to submit to Joe's demands he became verbally abusive, telling Hope that she was "pathetic" and that she should "lose her children by her first marriage and kill herself." Hope said that Joe began listing ways Hope could commit suicide. Hope told me that she was so distraught at the time that she reached into her purse, took several Xanax tablets (anxiety pills) and advised Joe that she was going into the house to call the police, her doctor, and an ambulance. Hope said that Joe, not wanting to be around when the police arrived, got back in his car and fled from Hope's residence.

Hope followed through on her threat to Joe that day and after several days in the hospital, returned home to find her house was a mess, as though it had been riffled through. Hope suspected Joe. Hope also said that Joe had been showing up at her home unannounced and would cut her grass while Hope locked herself in the house for fear of him. Now, I don't pretend to be able to read minds, but I suspect Joe wasn't cutting Hope's grass because he was a good guy. It's more likely that it was supposed to send a sideways message to Hope. What was the message? "I can still do what I want and I can still get to you," from Joe's perspective.

I took an offense report for Hope, obtained a written statement, and told Hope that the case would be turned over to our CID as several possible felonies had been committed, including: false imprisonment, aggravated assault, breaking and entering, and violation of Joe's bond conditions.

I left Hope after telling her that I would file my report that day and a detective would contact her soon to follow up on the incident. As I pulled out of Hope's driveway, I had the gut feeling that this would not be the last time I saw Hope, and I was right.

A few hours later, I received a radio call to respond to Hope's address on an unwanted subject. I'm not a rocket scientist, but I can put two and two together. I anticipated that I was about to meet Joe the Lawnmower Man.

As I pulled onto Hope's street I saw a man, matching Joe's description, in Hope's front yard cutting the grass. I approached the man and asked him to turn off his lawn mower. The man identified himself as Joe and I asked him if he was supposed to be there, given his bond conditions. Joe said that he knew he was not supposed to be there. I took Joe into custody, charged him with criminal trespass, and told him not to return to Hope's residence to pick up his truck and lawn mower without calling us for a standby officer.

Of course, when Joe was released from the Criminal Justice Center, where did he go? Yep, Joe went back to Hope's to get his truck and lawnmower without following my instructions and calling for a standby officer first. Some guys never learn, and Joe the Lawnmower Man was no exception.

Joe the Lawnmower Man is still cutting grass, but now he's cutting it for the county, and Hope finally has reason to exercise her name.

16

ALARM CALLS, 911 HANG-UPS, AND 911 OPEN LINES

It's the call you hate. The radio crackles with an alarm call and you have to answer it. You know the odds are ten to one that it is not serious or even a problem. It's usually nothing. A cat doing acrobatics from curtain rod to curtain rod sets off the alarm. Or a fumble-fingered employee hits the panic button while trying to stick his half-chewed gum under the counter. Papaw forgot the code. Sissy came home from college early and didn't know the new code. Let's be frank, most of the time, alarm calls are nuisance calls. Nothing really worth leaving your supper mid-bite to respond to, but you have no choice. "10-4," you respond.

Many larger agencies don't even answer calls generated from private alarm services. Those that still do are generally located in affluent communities where *everything* is life or death to rich folks.

Your duty as an officer is to check the residence or business. Then you leave a written warning in a door jamb or on the office manager's desk. If it's the fifth response to a false alarm or accidental activation, a fine is assessed to the tune of twenty-five dollars or so, depending upon your local ordinance.

In actuality, an alarm's best function is prevention—to frighten away a would-be burglar by making an ear-splitting, excruciatingly annoying racket so neighbors close by hear it and will do anything to make it stop, including calling the police or going outside and giving the offender the stink-eye.

Police officers don't rush to alarm calls unless the calls are initiated at a bank or convenience store that operates twenty-four hours per day. Now, I'm not saying that police officers meander to most alarm calls, but we don't usually place our lives, the lives of others, and the agency equipment at risk by running code to a business that accidently sets off its alarm every time a new employee is working his or her first day on the job. Responding to alarm calls is not a law enforcement priority and really is just a service to the community and property owner.

But, like everything else in policing, it's the odd, routine call that ends up being the one that could get you or someone else killed, so take nothing for granted, even on an alarm call. Every now and then, you respond to a call and encounter a crime in progress. You have to correctly and quickly discern between a night cleaning service and a janitor with a toilet brush in his hand versus a burglar with a gun in his hand. Making the correct decision has no room for error. Making the wrong decision can have life-changing implications for all involved.

It's one of the most harrowing calls for a dispatcher. The 911 dispatcher answers the ringing line and hears a brief soundbite that sounds like something from a horror movie, and then the line goes dead, or worse, the line remains open while the dispatcher listens to the horror unfold and is powerless to help the victim beyond sending available police units code 3.

Luckily, most of the time, the 911 hang-up call, sometimes called a 911 open-line call, is yet another nuisance call for the police officer. The best-case scenarios are that they are the result of unsupervised children who are playing on the telephone, a customer service representative working in a call center who has to dial a "9" to get an outside line, or a paralegal at a law firm trying desperately to send a fax from a machine they do not know how to operate.

But they are not all false alarms. The worst-case scenarios are literally cries for help. Someone may have been in the process of dialing for emergency assistance when their attacker pulled the entire phone and phone jack out of the wall, effectively disconnecting the line. If an attacker knocks a cell phone from the victim's hand after it has connected with 911, the line may be left open. Or maybe a clerk at a bank is being robbed and all the clerk can do without attracting the attention of the suspects is to take the phone off the hook, dial 911, and leave the line open hoping that the dispatcher at the 911 Call Center surmises that something is amiss and sends help. It could even be an elderly person in the desperate throes of a heart attack who can only manage to dial 911 before collapsing unconscious onto the floor.

The bottom line is that use of the emergency 911 prefix coupled with the unknown is reason enough for the officer to respond to find out what is going on and render assistance if needed. On the way, you should be checking the address that you are responding to for call history, to determine if emergency personnel have been to the address before, and what the nature of those calls were.

A 911 hang-up or open-line call in and of itself does not require an emergency response, but if a prior history exists that would lead an officer to believe that a crime is being committed or someone may have a medical emergency, you should bump up or step up your response to code 3. For example, an officer is dispatched on a 911 hang-up call, and when he discovers from checking the call history at this address that there have been several domestic disturbances there in the past, the response may be escalated. He would likely respond code 2, operating under the assumption that he is likely responding to another domestic disturbance, a call that would usually be dispatched as a code 2 or code 3 response.

Each time you respond to a call of this nature, you should be cautious in your approach and be extremely vigilant. Here's an example. An officer responding to a 911 hang-up call was surprised by a barefooted woman wearing pajamas sprinting toward the officer. The woman was obviously not armed, and was screaming and frightened. The front door to her home stood open, and as the officer approached he could see broken dinnerware and furniture in the living room area of the home. On entry, he discovered broken furniture, recently prepared food on the kitchen floor, along with broken dishes in the living room as though they'd been thrown, and a wall phone on the floor with bare wire extending from the wall where the phone jack once was.

The pajama-clad woman was a domestic violence victim and told the officer that she had just been in a physical confrontation with her husband. She stated that he had pulled the phone out of the wall when she tried to call 911 for help and then ran from the house, taking the family van to a local hotel. The victim knew this because her husband, the abuser, stomped off stating his intentions as he went.

Police located the suspect at the local hotel the victim said he would run to, identified his vehicle, checked the guest register with the night manager, secured an arrest warrant for the suspect, and obtained a key to the suspect's hotel room. Following his arrest, he was charged with aggravated assault and false imprisonment for holding the victim against her will and attempting to prevent her from dialing 911 for help.

Now we're in the age of technology and have to deal with 911 calls from cell phones that were dialed by accident while in someone's pocket, cars that are equipped with OnStar are moving when the call is received by dispatchers, and even malfunctioning alarm panels or advanced call center software that automatically dials "9" to access an outside line in order to return a customer's call.

Regardless, officers will continue to respond to these calls. Cooperation between local law enforcement, businesses, and the community, as well as education of the public, can go a long way to reducing the number of erroneous calls that police officers respond to on a daily basis.

17

WHITE-COLLAR CRIME, FRAUD, FORGERY, AND DECEIT

For years, people have batted around the clichéd term "victimless crime," which many generally identify and accept to be a fallacy. And, in my opinion, they're right. There is no such thing as a "victimless crime." Someone always suffers as a result of a criminal's illegal actions and white-collar crimes are no exception. From check forgery, check kiting (using a bad check to get money), and fraud, to deception, trickery, and subterfuge, someone always gets hurt financially and otherwise.

One of the worst displays I've ever seen of this as an investigator occurred on the heels of one of the worst natural disasters in the history of the United States, Hurricane Katrina, which struck Louisiana and surrounding states in the Gulf of Mexico in 2005. Katrina took the lives of almost two thousand people and did approximately $108 billion in damage. It was a mess, affecting many states in the southeast, even inland where no damage or fatalities occurred.

In my jurisdiction, we housed displaced families from the gulf region in emergency shelters set up in churches, vacant factories, and even high-school gymnasiums. We also sent our SWAT team to Mississippi to relieve officers who were working nonstop to aid devastated communities and protect property from looting.

So, you'd have to be a person belonging to the lowest common denominator to take advantage of funds and resources earmarked to aid the suffering, right? Well, let me introduce you to one such sick individual.

Helen was born with a silver spoon in her mouth in a nearby metropolitan city of about one million people. She never had to do for herself, and later in life she married a guy who wasn't the earner she thought he would be, a guy that she had managed to hook before he realized how crazy she really was. They had two kids, a boy and a girl, whom they should have never had because neither of them had the patience or the desire to be a parent.

When Helen's husband realized she was nuts, Helen left him and the kids and began her life of crime, because it goes without saying that she couldn't hold down a job or live the life of an indigent. So she embraced her maladies that included being a pathological liar, bipolar behaviors, and probable multiple personality disorder. She started selling valuable antiques after taking out insurance on them, then filing false police reports claiming they had been stolen so that she could collect twice their value. She made up crimes, like purse snatching, that she claimed to be a victim of, again filing false reports and then trying to recoup cash. She even rented cars, passed them off as her own, took out insurance on them, and then reported those vehicles stolen. Suffice it to say that insurance fraud and filing false police reports became her main income, but, of course, it didn't take us long to catch on to what she was doing.

When she discovered that we were on to her and she was about to be arrested, she disappeared. While we were looking for her, she evolved her money-making scheme and stooped to a new low: taking out a mailbox at a stamp store location in New Orleans, creating a fictitious business, and then filing for and collecting funds from the Federal Emergency Management Agency (FEMA) that were set aside for victims of Hurricane Katrina, not Helen.

The obvious mistake that Helen made was to go from committing felonies that fell under the jurisdiction of the state to defrauding a federal agency and violating federal law, punishable by doing time in federal prison, which is not a joke, I can assure you.

I went to work with an FBI (Federal Bureau of Investigation) agent and together we closed in on Helen. We got so close that she fled without taking all her paper evidence with her, and we were able to collect it from the hotel she had been living in on FEMA money. Her name and fingerprints were all over the documentation, and yes, it's true you can pull fingerprints from paper; actually, it's more accurate to say they can be developed on the paper you touch and then preserved with a fixative for examination, documentation with photography, and then display in a courtroom.

With the help of the FBI, we tracked Helen down again and she was taken into custody, charged at the federal level, and because this was the first time she had committed a federal offense, placed in a half-way house of the feds in Florida, where she was to do her time and get the mental help she needed.

But we're talking about Helen here. Because security at the half-way house was minimal, she walked out one day and started committing fraud and crimes of deception with paper, just like she had been doing when she got caught. Only this time, she was violating her federal, in-house detention. She was tracked down by the US Marshal's service as an escapee from federal prison, charged with her new crimes, and then sent to the real, federal big house.

Unfortunately, while our problems ended with Helen, they were just beginning with her husband and the children he was left with caring for as a single parent. They, the kids, didn't fall far from the family tree, and it wasn't long before they were in juvenile detention and children's services were monitoring the family. Sad really, but you haven't heard anything yet.

You have to give them a certain amount of credit. People who commit fraud are often very creative people, and it causes an honest person to wonder how they come up with these wild ideas to score cash, products, and services through manipulation, deception, and deceit. Those are all excellent and legitimate questions. The easy answer to them is that committing fraud is the career these individuals have chosen. They sit around all day long between committing each crime and do nothing but fart around and think of ways to make their next mark. They are dedicated professionals. It just happens that their profession is illegal and involves victimizing honest, hard-working people.

I was assigned a case one day as a detective that involved a woman who was passing bad checks in town on a business that didn't exist, not unlike Helen. There was a difference, though: where Helen had actually opened an actual checking account at a bank for her nonexistent business, this lady had gone to an office supply store, bought commercial check printing paper, and was using the local library's computer lab (open to the public) to print the bad payroll checks on the bogus business. But there was a significant flaw in her execution. She wasn't using check writing software, but a word processing program at the library instead. So she had to format the printing manually for each check, and let's just say she wasn't the sharpest knife in the drawer, nor did she have an accounting degree or background in payroll.

At the bottom of a check is a line of numbers, referred to in the banking industry as the MICR line (pronounced mick-er). The magnetic ink character recognition (MICR) line isn't just any old jumble of numbers, and the ink used to print it is magnetic so that it can be read by special machines. That special ink doesn't come in your household printer cartridge, and the numbers correspond to a routing number, an account number, a check number, and also have special characters setting each number apart from the next. Suffice it to say that our suspect didn't know or understand the importance of a MICR line and did a bad job of recreating one. One look at the check by an investigator or a banking/accounting/payroll professional and you would know it was a forgery.

Like Helen, when this lady started getting a little warm (realized she was about to get caught), she skipped town, abandoning a room at a chain hotel near the interstate where she had been living with several "rescued animals" and her eight-year-old developmentally disabled son in utter filth. And I don't just mean a little bit of dust. They had been in the room for months, had never taken out the trash or picked up after the animals, and the room was rife with decaying fecal matter everywhere, along with rotting food and other trash. It was so bad that I had to suit up like I was going into a homicide scene where multiple bodies had been discovered and had been there for a while just cooking down in the summer heat. I donned a DuPont Tyvek suit (made of flash-spun, high-density polyethylene, which creates a unique, nonwoven material), gloves, and booties, and even had to wear a respirator, just to retrieve the evidence that she left behind, and there was a lot of it.

I caught up to her and her son down the road a bit, and needless to say, a confession was out of the question with her, as she was mentally ill like Helen. She could not differentiate between a lie and the truth, so everything that came out of her mouth, in her mixed-up mind, was accurate. But I had the evidence, she was convicted, her son was placed in a foster home (which was surely better than that hotel room), and hopefully, she got the help and medication she needed.

If that story wasn't bad enough, imagine someone so low that she would create a family that didn't exist and then tell her coworkers that her made-up children were suffering from a rare disease and that she needed help financially for their medical care. The coworkers, feeling bad for her, actually started a drive to collect money for this lady's diseased, nonexistent children, which she gladly accepted without giving it a second thought. She had no moral compass whatsoever.

Interestingly enough, this lady came to our attention when she was working at a soft pretzel kiosk in our shopping mall. I received a call from an individual who thought someone had hacked her credit card account and was running up charges on it; perhaps someone had captured the number using a skimming device that had been attached to a legitimate credit card terminal unbeknownst to the retailer, but at this time, skimming was new, and there weren't a lot of cases out there using this technology. The card owner still had possession of the credit card, so actual use of the physical card could be ruled out. That said, with the help of the card holder we came up with a narrow window when this had occurred and uncovered where she had used her card legitimately during that time period.

It didn't take long to figure out what was going on. One call to the owner of the soft pretzel kiosk at the mall and an inquiry as to who was scheduled to work at that time on that date, and the pieces started to come together. Turns out, the store owner was in the process of updating his cash register software so that the full number of a customer's credit card wouldn't appear on the cash register terminal or paper receipt when a purchase was made. He had upgraded the software at all of his locations except the kiosk at the mall, and guess who was working the day my victim's credit card number was stolen? Yep, the aforementioned lady. As soon as the owner looked at the old employee schedule, the story about her nonexistent children and her little fundraising drive came out. A few days later, she was invited to the stock room of the store by her manager to obtain an item for use in the kiosk and I was there, waiting with handcuffs for her. Her soft-pretzel-making days were over, and so were her days as a parent.

18

VIOLENT FELONIES

Make no mistake, a violent assault with a weapon on an individual that threatens grievous bodily harm or death while in the commission of a crime or in isolation is a very personal incident. It's the category of crime that law enforcement professionals take the most seriously.

Crimes that fall within the category of violent felonies are broad-ranging, from aggravated assault and aggravated robbery all the way to aggravated kidnapping, especially aggravated vehicular homicide, murder, aggravated rape of a child, and even criminal exposure to Human Immunodeficiency Virus (HIV). Do these sound personal enough to you? Yes, me too!

The simple fact is that nothing is more precious than a human life. To threaten or take the life of another human being with a weapon of any kind should be and is addressed swiftly and to the full extent of the law in the United States.

As a police officer, you will, if you do the job long enough, have your life threatened. You will be placed in life-threatening positions, and you will step into harm's way in the defense of another. That's the gig, like it or not. You will also be exposed to crimes of violence before, during, and after the fact, again, again, and again. That too, is what you signed up for. So you need to consider whether or not you are prepared to accept the risks and consequences associated with performing the duty of a police officer every day you don the uniform and step out into public with that badge pinned to your breast. And not only is it incumbent on you to consider these facts, you should also consider the feelings and opinions of your loved ones, because they will live, suffer, and sacrifice alongside you for the choice you make to enter this profession.

Merriam-Webster's Collegiate Dictionary, tenth edition, defines "aggravate" as "to make heavy, to make worse, more serious, or more severe," and there can be no doubt that dragging a box cutter forty-seven centimeters diagonally across someone's exposed chest and back or throwing an infant down a flight of metal stairs outside of a fleabag motel is serious or severe!

Both of those crimes really happened; I responded to both of them and many more like them during my career as a cop, and I can tell you without any equivocation that they were difficult to handle and emotionally taxing for me and all of the parties involved. Crimes against children are especially difficult and really get a police officer's blood boiling, but you have to maintain your self-control and professionalism, no matter how difficult the incident was, is, or becomes.

Not long into my time in law enforcement, I received a call to respond to a disturbance in progress at a local trailer park. The nature of the disturbance was not clear at the time of the dispatch, but we did know that it involved an edged weapon and that grievous bodily injury had already occurred.

My zone (area) partner and I responded code 3 to the call and on the way I went over in my head what I had learned at the police academy and in field training concerning response to edged-weapons attacks. First and foremost is officer safety, because if I don't survive the response to or the call itself, then I am of no use to anyone. Second, when confronted with any kind of edged weapon, from a tactical standpoint, you (the officer) need to keep a safe, reactionary gap of at least twenty-one feet between you and the suspect. If the distance is any closer, then the officer will not have enough time to react by unholstering their sidearm (handgun) and potentially firing it. Just in case you were debating it, know that an assault with an edged weapon is considered a deadly force assault, and the recommended response to meet that level of resistance is the "Use of Deadly Force."

When I arrived at the entrance to the trailer park, my zone partner right behind me, I observed the subject I believed to be the victim hunched over with a blood-soaked towel covering his t-shirt and abdomen. He was wearing blue jeans, and they too were completely soaked with blood, so I knew he was in bad shape and needed immediate medical attention. I radioed my partner who was just behind me and let him know that I was proceeding to the scene of the incident and asked him to standby with the victim until help arrived. It didn't appear that the victim was armed, and he was hurt so badly that I felt that my zone partner should handle him until additional backup units arrived on scene to assist.

As I pulled into the cul-de-sac where the incident occurred and the trailer was located, a male subject exited the front entrance to the residence and started walking quickly toward me. I threw my patrol car into park, jumped out, and immediately ordered the subject, whom I believed to be the suspect, to stay where he was! I asked him if he had been involved in the incident and if he was in possession of the weapon used, to which he replied in the affirmative. Then without any prompting, he stated, "I'm the one who cut him, and I'd do it again!" Well, if that isn't an admission, I don't know what is. We in the profession also refer to that as a "spontaneous utterance." It certainly doesn't take a rocket scientist to arrive at the conclusion that this is the guy we were looking for, and he has admitted his involvement in the incident. The details of the incident would still need to be sorted out, complete with written statements from all parties involved.

Interestingly enough, the suspect didn't appear to have a scratch on him, leading me to believe that the victim had got the worst of it and the altercation had been pretty one-sided.

I placed the suspect in a position of disadvantage, having him turn around and get down on his knees, cross one ankle over the other, and place his hands on the top of his head. Not only does this give me the upper hand tactically should he decide to jump up and attack me, but it also makes it safer for me to take him into custody when my backup arrives, which is what we did.

The suspect who did the "cutting" had a box cutter in his front pocket that was loaded with a brand new razor blade he had installed that day before leaving the warehouse where he worked. So it was surgically sharp and could open up a person's skin like a scalpel in an operating room. I later learned that not only was the victim opened up from the front, but also from the back with equal ferocity. Details like this become important in a felony investigation and provide detectives with clues as to the order of events as they relate to the incident.

In order to understand why this incident occurred, it's important to have knowledge of the events that led up to its initiation; that way, you can put the situation into proper context. You'll also be able to understand the actions of each party during the incident.

In this case, both parties knew each other and had previous history (not good history), though they were not related by blood or otherwise. Let's just say they knew each other from the neighborhood, and let's call them Sam and Ralph for the purposes of this narrative.

Two years prior to our response, Sam, the guy whose chest had been opened up by Ralph during their altercation, had kidnapped Ralph's wife and child and transported them to an adjoining county, where he held them by force over an entire weekend. Sam eventually kicked Ralph's kid out of the car at gunpoint, but kept Ralph's wife, which was the real object of his crime, or shall we say, "affection."

Finally, after being pursued religiously by law enforcement, Sam came to the conclusion that he should return to our county and city, release Ralph's wife on the side of the road, and ditch his shotgun in the dumpster of a local convenience store. And this is just what Sam did. Not long after that, we caught up with him, and the jig was up, so to speak. Sam was convicted and sent "up the river," or in professional terms, to the state penitentiary for his crime. But before Sam could be dragged out of the courtroom, Ralph had time to deliver a threat, one that he would reiterate just a few weeks prior to our call. It went something like, "Sam, if you ever come near my wife or my family again, I will kill you!" It's pretty hard to misinterpret that message, and I am sure that Sam got the gist of it.

Fast forward several years, and Sam is paroled from the state penitentiary, whereupon he immediately returns to his hometown and my jurisdiction. Sam heads straight for the local watering hole (bar) and, lo and behold, he runs into Ralph and his wife there. Now, if Sam had, as we say in the South, "a lick of sense," he would have turned around and walked out of that joint, recalling Ralph's warning, but as fate would have it, you can't teach stupid. Yep, he walked right over to Ralph and his wife, stuck out his hand in front of Ralph, and stated that he was "sorry" for kidnapping Ralph's wife and child at gunpoint years earlier, and "could they let bygones be bygones and become friends?" Well, that offer of renewed friendship went over about like a ton of bricks with Ralph, as you might imagine. Ralph stood up and reiterated his previous warning to Sam in a voice what was audible to everyone in the establishment. So Sam, taking

Ralph's meaning, retreated to the bar to drown his sorrows and lament the loss of his misdirected love toward Ralph's wife.

Fast forward again, this time just two weeks after the encounter at the local bar. Sam gets off work on a sunny, summer afternoon and heads home to the trailer park, where he proceeds to drown his work week with a bottle of ninety-proof whiskey. About halfway into the fifth, he decides that it would be a good idea if he attempted to patch things up with Ralph and his wife again. So he jumps into the driver's seat of his truck, bringing the bottle with him, and careens on over to Ralph's trailer, where he finds the front door open and screen door closed.

Sam jumps out of his rusted hulk and up onto the front porch of Ralph's trailer, flings open the front door, and enters the living room where Ralph and his wife are reclining together on the sofa watching television. On the coffee table is Ralph's new box cutter with the blade he had just replaced that day. You know, the one from the warehouse. Ralph jumps up to meet Sam, who just entered his trailer uninvited, and Sam, realizing he has made a mistake, figures he should get the first punch in and coldcocks Ralph in the face in his own living room. Well, Ralph grabs his box cutter with his right hand and the collar of Sam's t-shirt with his left hand, flips the box cutter open, and slashes Sam diagonally from the bottom left of his torso to the upper right, opening Sam up so deep that his intestines were falling out of his body cavity. But wait, Ralph wasn't finished with Sam.

Ralph, intent to make good on his previous warning/threat, pushed Sam out of the trailer through the front screen door, turning him around in the process, and then slashed him across the back with the box cutter, the same way he had opened him up in the front. Sam fell off the front porch in shock, but with his adrenaline pumping managed to stand up and make a run for the entrance to the trailer park, guts in hand. Heaven only knows where he got the towel we saw him with. Ralph, fortunately, didn't pursue Sam, but left him with another warning, "Don't come back again!" I'm sure that Sam finally internalized that message, though it must have been made harder with his insides on the outside.

So now you are up to speed. I won't go into all the details and bore you with the rest of the investigation and facts, but suffice it to say that Sam, who was initially thought to be the victim, ended up being the suspect, and Ralph was found to have acted in self-defense. I'm sure you're probably wondering what happened to Sam. Did he survive the box cutter attack? Was he charged with a crime/s?

Well, here's the answer. Yes, thanks to an outstanding response by fire, EMS, and medical personnel at the hospital, Sam did survive. Sam had a lot of intestinal fortitude, didn't he? That's what we refer to as "gallows humor" in law enforcement.

Was he charged? The answer is no. We could've charged him, but you have to realize that Ralph was no fan of law enforcement, had a bit of a criminal record himself, and preferred to handle his own problems. He really didn't want to participate in Sam's prosecution and send him back to the pen, which would make Ralph feel like a rat and less than a man in his mind. And Sam, he was just grateful to be alive, and when he sobered up he concluded that he had it coming to him. So, the docs stapled Sam up across the front and the back and sent him home to the trailer park. But, you know, that tattoo of Sam's last name across his chest never quite matched up again after Ralph separated it with a box cutter that day.

Some guys just like to fight. Before I became a police officer and during my tenure as a cop, I knew a lot of them. But I never knew a kid who loved to fight more than Brandon. This young man loved to fight so much that he carried a football player's mouth guard around in the front pocket of his blue jeans, just so he wouldn't have any teeth knocked out if a rival was lucky enough to land a punch to his jaw. Brandon literally went around town looking for someone to fight, and if that wasn't enough, his free time was spent crafting crude impact (blunt force trauma) weapons to use on his opponents if his fists just weren't enough.

Brandon was the son of a registered nurse who had a drinking problem she indulged at night and on the weekends. She was a functioning alcoholic, and Brandon had a brother who was just above functional literacy. So life wasn't the best for Brandon. To make matters worse, Brandon had inherited his mother's drinking problem, but in his youthful exuberance, he didn't manage it as well as she did. Finally, Brandon liked to use cocaine, a stimulant that tends to give someone a lot of energy and a false sense of invincibility. So you have a pretty good idea of who we were dealing with.

Over the years, Brandon was in and out of trouble as a juvenile, and once he became an adult, he continued to have run-ins with law enforcement, but usually just alcohol-fueled misdemeanors that would land him in county lockup for a few days, nothing serious. We warned Brandon each time that one of these days, if he wasn't careful, he was going to cross the line and end up going to prison, but he never was much on listening to the advice of others, or he just wasn't capable of remembering the advice past his time in the county jail. Because as soon as he got out, he started killing off his brain cells again with alcohol.

Well, sure enough, one weekend when I was the on-call detective, the phone rang at home. I was called in to investigate an aggravated robbery where a shotgun was put to the back of a kid's head behind the ice cream shop after he completed his shift, all for about three dollars in tip money that the teenager kept in the ashtray of his car. The teen got a good look at the suspect, his clothing, and some distinctive tattoos he was sporting, which was not only a good observation on the part of the brave teen, but would be an important piece of evidence. The victim also mentioned that the suspect had gotten into a white sport utility vehicle and fled the scene with two other guys.

On my way into the city, I was monitoring my police radio when a second call came out, where a suspect matching the description of the first one placed a woman at gunpoint and demanded her pocketbook. The second call was in proximity to the first one. So it looked like a pattern was beginning to develop; the suspect was running around town randomly robbing anyone he thought he could victimize without too much trouble.

I had a bit of good fortune on my side that night, because the second victim recognized the suspect and called him out by name, which alarmed the suspect and caused him to run away without the lady's purse. The lady was so close to the suspect that not only did she recognize him and remember what he was wearing, but she identified what was thought by the first victim to be a shotgun, but was in reality a broom handle. Sound like anyone we know? Yep, you guessed it, Brandon.

So, I made a little trip with a couple of patrol units over to Brandon's mother's house and made contact with his brother, who without any prompting from me other than "Have you seen Brandon tonight? And what was he wearing?" provided me with a description that matched both victims' descriptions of the clothes Brandon was wearing. Brandon wasn't at home, but I left with the caveat that if he came home, his brother should call us as soon as possible.

I was able to relax a little bit at this point, because now I knew that Brandon didn't have a shotgun, or any gun for that matter, but I was still concerned, mostly for Brandon, that he would hold someone up who had a concealed handgun carry permit and would shoot him cold on the spot. Brandon was stupid, but I didn't believe he would kill someone intentionally, and as a police officer, you really never wish death on anyone. Not even Brandon.

While patrol units kept an eye out for Brandon, I drove to the magistrate's office with the first victim's statement in hand and my personal observations gathered from the second victim and Brandon's brother. I took out a warrant on Brandon for aggravated robbery, because even though he didn't use a gun, the broom handle was a weapon, and when it's stuck in the back of your neck from behind and someone states "don't turn around, just hand me your money," you might reasonably believe the end of that round broom handle to be the barrel of a shotgun—which is what Brandon was counting on.

With a warrant on file, I began looking for Brandon again, and the hunt continued into the next morning. Fourteen hours into the search, dispatch/communications received a call from Brandon's brother, who said Brandon had just returned home. We converged on the house and knocked on the front door. Brandon opened it wide and was ordered by the closest detective to "grab some dirt," which in cop slang means hit the ground, bubba. Brandon complied, but he kept wanting to turn his head up and give the officers the evil eye, which they did not appreciate. Brandon's unwillingness to keep his head down was met with a shotgun to his nose. Brandon got the point, so to speak, and put his head back down.

I got Brandon back to the station and began the long process of trying to drag the story of the previous night's events out of him. He told me that he owed a couple of drug dealers some money and that they had approached him the previous afternoon, forced him to join them, and said they wanted him to knock some people over. According to Brandon, they told him that he couldn't stop until they had their money. Those were the guys in the white SUV, presumably. But Brandon insisted that he was not the one who held the victims at gunpoint, that he was just riding in the SUV with the guys, and that they were responsible. Of course, either way, gunman or not, he was involved and his story was incriminating. Fortunately for us, and unfortunately for Brandon, he was on probation for previous misdemeanor drug convictions, and he had been using cocaine at the time of the robbery, by his own admission. So in addition to his involvement in the robbery, he had violated his probation, which meant no bail for Brandon. I could keep him locked up until the trial in circuit court on the robbery charges.

When the day came for the trial, the hearing was short; Brandon pled guilty and was sentenced to serve out the time on his probation violation and his aggravated robbery conviction in the state penitentiary. Sentences of two years or less are usually served in the county jail, but sentences of three years or more will land you in the "big house."

Fast forward a year and a half, and sure enough, Brandon was trying to get paroled, which meant we'd be dealing with him again. But the ADA had other ideas and wrote a letter to the parole board, as did I. As a result, Brandon's parole was denied, and he continues to serve time, as far as I know, and our community is a little safer for it—and frankly, so is Brandon.

19

DEATH SCENES

Walking into a Nightmare

If you do this job long enough, sooner or later you will come face to face with the cold, often harsh reality that people die every day. Sometimes good people die at the hands of bad people, in heartbreaking accidents, or by their own hand. Deaths are usually handled by the detectives of the Homicide Division, but as a patrol officer, you might be the first responder to a death in a motor vehicle accident or when doing a welfare check on someone requested by a family member or friend. Or you might be called upon to secure the scene of a homicide.

These calls are sad, tragic, and they affect you every single time you encounter them. You will remember the victims and the circumstances of their deaths in detail, forever.

If you aren't emotionally ready to respond to these calls or to come face to face with your own issues surrounding mortality, then you don't need to be a police officer. You need to find another line of work, and I mean now! Don't waste any more time in law enforcement or the precious time of law enforcement professionals who are willing and somewhat equipped to handle death. If you stay, you run the risk of becoming mentally and emotionally crippled.

Remember, you are there to protect and serve the citizens of your community, dead or alive. Part of the job of law enforcement professionals is to try to ensure that Grandma is viewed by her grandchildren at the funeral home in a somewhat natural state and not hanging from a stereo speaker cable across a bi-folding closet door just one foot above the bedroom floor. It's the right thing to do for Grandma and, best thing you can do for the grieving family. They shouldn't have to see the blood running down Grandma's chin that she aspirated while strangling to death, connecting to what appears to be a frozen stream of blood reaching down to a bright red puddle on the beige carpet. They shouldn't see the children's cafeteria chair she kicked out from under her lying turned over across the room, the very same chair they sat in so many times while coloring with Grandma, who will never color with them again.

Fortunately, with the exception of motor vehicle accidents that end in a fatality, patrol officers don't have to linger over a death scene. It's usually the detectives who spend the long, grueling, and gut-wrenching hours processing evidence at the scene and attending the autopsy at the state medical examiner's (ME) office. For the patrol officer, your responsibility usually revolves around notifying your supervisor if CID is needed, keeping a log of people coming in and out of the death scene, and writing the initial report.

The two types of death scenes you'll encounter in law enforcement can be categorized as unexpected and expected. Unexpected deaths are homicides, suicides, fatal accidents, violent deaths, drug and alcohol overdoses, deaths where the victim is young, or deaths where an unknown medical condition is responsible for ending someone's life.

Expected deaths include hospice deaths; deaths at a medical center; deaths that occur with a licensed nurse, doctor, or caregiver in attendance; or deaths resulting from chronic or terminal illnesses that are attended by someone familiar with the individual's medical history and where there is no obvious foul play.

It usually falls to the responding officer and police agency to report on any and all deaths in their jurisdiction. Some agencies only respond to unexpected deaths, depending on their policies and the laws of their city, county, and state.

Again, the thing to remember here and prepare for is the personal effect that working a death scene will have on you. If you have kids and you respond to the death of a child, you'll naturally think about your own kids. If you respond to the death of an elderly person and you have elderly parents or grandparents, you will think about them. And so it goes. You do not and cannot totally compartmentalize your work from your personal life.

Any exposure to a death scene is significant, and it will have a lasting effect on you. If you are operating under the assumption that you won't be affected, that you will tough your way through it or tamp it all down without consequence, stop deluding yourself. You won't. You may do that successfully for a while, but eventually it will catch up to you.

Officers should see a counselor at least once a year and do a self-assessment on how they are feeling emotionally on a regular basis. Otherwise, you'll end up being an alcoholic, a drug addict, an abuser, or engaged in some other form of negative, self-medicating behavior in an effort to cope with the mounting effect of violence and death you encounter routinely on the job.

Don't believe me? Okay, I'll be by to visit you as an inpatient at your local psychiatric hospital, or even worse, I'll be attending your funeral after you put your duty weapon in your mouth and blow the back of your head off in your patrol car at the end of your shift. Don't let that happen! Talk about your feelings and what you experience with your spiritual advisor, a trained and licensed counselor, psychiatrist, or even a good friend. You'll be glad you did. The life you save may be your own.

Death is personal, and depending on your belief system, this life may or may not be the only one you and your loved ones will experience. You will also be forced to come to terms with your own mortality and the shortened life expectancy of a police officer. No one wants to die or to deal with death. That's why police officers stand in the gap with firefighters, EMS personnel, medical examiners, death investigators, and morticians. So get a good counselor and don't be afraid to see that counselor on a regular basis as you face death on the job.

It was a Saturday afternoon in the middle of one very hot summer. I was standing in a jewelry store, shopping for a charm bracelet for our daughter when my cell phone rang. It was the police department and I was the on-call detective, so I had to answer. Dispatch connected me to one of our patrol sergeants on the day shift, who advised he had an active death scene at a truck stop near the interstate and it was getting ready to pour rain. What should he do?

I advised the shift supervisor that I would be on my way and in the meantime he should secure the scene with crime scene tape, assign a patrol officer to protect the perimeter, and document anyone in or out of the tape, authorized personnel only. I also told him to have a patrol officer obtain a tarp from the truck stop and cover the car where the decedent was in the event it started to rain before I got there in an effort to preserve the scene.

When I arrived at the automobile parking area of the truck stop and stepped out of my unmarked car, which I parked outside of the large perimeter that had been taped off by patrol, I could already smell the decedent, or rather the stench of accelerated decomposition. It had been over one hundred degrees every day that week, and the parking lot was steaming, causing the decedent in the small car with the windows up to decompose at a faster rate than normal.

I approached the car and could see flies already laying eggs in the decedent's mouth and eyelids, and his skin had already begun to slough, slip off of the muscle and bone, or sag. I also noticed that the keys were in the ignition and the ignition was in the on position, but the car battery was dead and the gas gauge was on empty. So it was logical to assume that the car had been running at the decedent's time of death and had run out of gas. I also observed an almost empty bottle of vodka on the passenger seat, two pill bottles (one empty), and a newspaper with ads for call girls. I began in the usual way by photographing the scene and interviewing witnesses and employees of the truck stop.

I learned that the car had been parked there for a few days and that several women—lot lizards (prostitutes who frequent truck stops and truckers)—had been seen getting in and out of the vehicle the decedent was occupying. The decedent had last been seen alive the previous night, when one of these women was observed by a truck stop employee exiting the vehicle and crying as she ran off. The car was running with the headlights on, according to the employee who observed the woman leaving the scene.

After interviewing witnesses and photographing the scene, I began to process the car and collect evidence while waiting on a field investigator from the ME's office to arrive. I found more empty alcohol containers under the seat of the car and an old driver's license that I believed belonged to the decedent in the glove box. The name on the license matched the name of the prescription bottles I found in the front seat. The bottle containing pills held blood pressure medication that had no street value, but the empty pill bottle had contained Ambien (a sleeping pill with illicit uses and street value). I noted that the pills had not been consumed according to the prescriber's instructions, because there had been sixty pills and the script had been filled only one day before my call out. Additionally, the suspect's wallet was missing. Strange.

I theorized that the suspect was drinking, had called the prostitute, and had died of an overdose or natural causes, after which the call girl arrived, found the decedent dead in his car, and began to cry, but she wasn't upset enough to run away before stealing the decedent's Ambien and wallet, which little did she know contained no money or credit cards that weren't maxed out. I would find that out later in my investigation.

I located the victim's brother, and when I finished at the scene with the ME and evidence processing, I went to meet him with the police department's chaplain. It turns out that the decedent was a career alcoholic and as a result had encountered trouble holding a job. Their elderly parents had bought the decedent the car he was found in, and he had been living in it since he had been kicked out of their other brother's house for coming in drunk in the middle of the night, knocking over household items, and waking up their children. Later, he would return to his brother's house and burglarize it, so you get the picture here. His brother identified him from the photographs taken at the scene.

Two weeks later the ME's office returned their results: the decedent had died of a massive heart attack, probably before the prostitute arrived, and did not have medication in his system, again, pointing to the theft of the medication by the prostitute. We were never able to identify the prostitute through evidence collected at the scene, so we'll never know exactly what happened, but we do know that it was not a homicide scene and that the decedent died of natural causes, after which he became the victim of a theft.

The most difficult death scenes you will ever work as a detective are those involving young adults or children. It was a weekday morning when I was called to such a scene at an apartment complex in our city. The decedent was a young Indian woman, approximately twenty-one years old, who was occupying an apartment with five other young Indian women. They were all computer programmers who were in the United States on a work visa and were sharing a one-bedroom apartment to save money for their families in India.

The young women were all sleeping on the floor of the living room the night before my callout and had earlier been out to dinner and shopping at a local mall. The decedent's friends told me that she had been complaining all day of a headache and that in the middle of the night she woke up sweating profusely and vomiting. Then finally, early in the morning of my callout, she had sat bolt upright in her sleeping bag, screamed out the Bengali word for "mother," and then fell backward and began aspirating blood and saliva from her mouth and nose. EMS was called, and she was rushed to the hospital where she was pronounced dead on arrival (DOA). I processed the scene at the apartment and headed for the hospital.

When I arrived at the hospital, the ER waiting area was filled with the decedent's friends and coworkers. I made contact with the ER physician attending the decedent and then took the photographs I had to take. I have to say, it was pretty tough to unzip the body bag the decedent had been placed in and photograph this beautiful young Indian woman who still had the trach protruding from her mouth.

I composed myself, zipped the bag back up, and made contact with her friends, who were very kind and very helpful in reaching her family in India, explaining why the autopsy had to be performed before we could return the body of their daughter to India and the time it would take to do this.

When an unexpected death of an otherwise healthy young person occurs and that death is unattended, the body must be autopsied to determine the cause of death, and until that cause is determined, the case is treated as a homicide investigation.

To add to an already disconcerting case, I was contacted by the ME's office a few days later as a precaution. Preliminary autopsy results indicated that the decedent died of a brain bleed that was so sudden and severe that it literally pushed blood from the brain and head of the decedent down into the decedent's spinal column. Because of the decedent's country of origin and because India has many active cases of contagious meningitis, the ME's office wanted to make me aware that it is possible I could have been infected while processing the scene, despite my precautions. So, suffice it to say, it was a scary situation on top of a really difficult case.

Fortunately, autopsy results several weeks later revealed that the decedent was not suffering from contagious meningitis, but rather had a colloid cyst on the third ventricle of her brain that had ruptured, explaining the brain bleed and the headache she had complained of. I learned subsequently that such cysts can be in the brain from the time of birth, and that people with these cysts could live their entire life not knowing they were there until they had a head injury that required a CT scan, thus revealing the cyst, or, as in this case, until the cyst ruptured, if it ever ruptured.

Death can be strange, unexpected, unusual, and confounding. It can come early in, in the middle of, or late in life. It can take anyone from any background and under any circumstances. It is certain that it will come to each of us, but usually uncertain as to how or when.

It was late one night when my phone rang, calling me in to another death scene. I say death scene because it's not always obvious whether you are going to be working a homicide, suicide, or natural death at the outset, and patrol is not trained to determine the difficult ones. That's where CID and death investigators come in.

In this case, a neighbor had noticed that newspapers were piling up in his neighbor's driveway. The neighbor was known to suffer from schizophrenia, but never missed getting his paper every morning. Patrol responded to the residence initially, and after receiving no response, they forced entry and discovered the decedent. They backed out and radioed for CID.

When I arrived and entered the scene, a 1970s-style ranch house, all of the wall heaters in the residence were on and set on high. It was incredibly warm and, of course, as you might expect, you could smell death. I made my way to the rear of the home, photographing the scene as I went, and entered the bedroom of the decedent. He was stretched out on the bed and had been there for some time. His facial features were not recognizable from other pictures in the home, and his body was extremely bloated from the gases created by the decomposition process.

There was a trashcan in close proximity to the decedent, and from its contents, it was obvious that he had been sick. There were no signs of foul play. The difficult part of this case was positively identifying the decedent. While it was likely that we knew who this was, it was impossible for us to say with a large degree of certainty due to the decomposition that had already taken place. We would need a positive identification from a relative that knew the decedent well enough to recognize him even in this state. Of course, the ME's office could also confirm with dental records if he had any, but in this case he did not. He was suffering from schizophrenia and had been all of his life, and was afraid of going to the dentist. So he never did. We did find a relative, and a positive identification was made.

After the ME arrived and finished processing the scene, it was time to remove the body. You may recall that I referenced the bloating. When the attendants from the ME's office lifted the body from the bed, it ruptured like a balloon, releasing gases and fluid. Suffice it to say that if you intend to be a criminal investigator, you will need to have a strong stomach. Many investigators use nose plugs or smear Vicks VapoRub under the openings of their nostrils. Some even go as far as using ammonia poppers to help with the smell, but I have always just gutted it out, believing that all of my senses need to be awake when conducting an investigation. Also, I convinced myself that this would help me to get used to it and get over that sick feeling. I did get over it and got used to it, but you will never forget the smell of death and will always know it immediately after you have been exposed to it as an investigator.

"I asked him what happened, lieutenant, but he wasn't talking," I said. The lieutenant chuckled at the comment as we crossed the crime scene tape and made our way to the body lying next to the fence.

If you think my comment sounds crass, insensitive, or even inappropriate, I would invite you to walk a homicide or suicide scene in my shoes, then revisit my remark and determine if you still feel the same way.

I had been a detective, assigned to the Major Crimes Unit of CID for just over a year when I made that statement to my lieutenant. It was late in the afternoon and I was about to leave the office when the call crackled over the loudspeakers. I was already grabbing my gear when our sergeant called over the cube walls for everyone present in our unit to gather around. We already knew where we were going.

Less than five minutes later we were on our way to a parking area of a large agricultural arena, where we were advised by communications that we'd find a male subject, possibly a suicide victim, lying on the ground unresponsive. Even without EMS running a strip (a printout from a heart monitor), we knew he would be dead.

Patrol officers arrived just ahead of us, accompanied by patrol supervisors, and they had secured the scene for us. My sergeant arrived moments before me with the on-call detective for the week, who was already taking crime scene photos. The Crash Investigation and Reconstruction Team (CIRT) was on the way, as they were not only assigned to investigate accidents but also diagram crime scenes for us.

I ducked under the crime scene tape and approached the decedent. He was an older, white male subject wearing overalls, a button-down shirt, and cowboy boots. He was balding, and I could already see the presence of lividity on the crown of his head. I didn't need EMS to run a strip. He was dead. There was a Remington 870 Wingmaster shotgun lying on the ground next to the victim. Right away, it was obvious that something wasn't right. There are certain things a detective expects to see at a suicide scene where the death is by shotgun, but this scene was different for a number of reasons.

First of all, there was no obvious entry wound. Second, there were only minimal signs of blood on the outer clothing of the decedent (just a little stain on the front of his overalls). There was no spent shotgun shell on the ground. The action of the shotgun was open, meaning in the position just before a round is pushed to the chamber or just after a shot is fired and the operator has opened the bolt to eject an empty shell. The port side of the shotgun was to the ground and not visible. The good news was that the safety on the shotgun was off. If it were on, that would have indicated that it would have been impossible for the decedent to have shot himself.

Without moving the body or shotgun, it would be impossible to confirm that the man lying motionless on the ground had shot himself. On a homicide or suicide scene, the diagram must be completed before a body can be moved or evidence gathered. Additionally, only the ME can move the body, and she was not on scene. So we could not say with any assurance that this individual had committed suicide. With that in mind, we opted to treat this as a homicide investigation until evidence of a suicide emerged. In most cases, the body tells the story, and this case would be no different.

Shortly following our arrival, the crime scene unit and Incident Command Vehicle (ICV) arrived on scene. The ICV is a very large, specially equipped, motorhome-like vehicle which serves as both an operations center and place to get out of extreme weather. If you do this job long enough, you soon learn that crime scenes usually present themselves in the worst of conditions. On this day in February, the temperature started out around sixty degrees Fahrenheit, but by dusk we had dropped into the thirties with a wind chill below freezing.

While we waited for the ME to arrive, additional detectives arrived on scene, and the division of responsibilities began. Witnesses had been located at a construction site across the road from the crime scene. However, they only heard a muffled shot and saw the decedent lying on the ground. They did not witness the victim shoot himself or being shot by someone else. The good news was that they did locate the decedent's driver's license on the dashboard of an SUV in the parking lot. Two detectives were sent to interview the witnesses and take statements while two detectives were sent with the police department's chaplain to the residence of the decedent to notify his next of kin. They took a photograph of the decedent with them in order to obtain a positive identification.

In the meantime, registrations were run on all vehicles in the parking lot near the crime scene. Remaining detectives scoured the area for additional evidence that might provide insight into what happened on this cold afternoon.

It wasn't long before numbered placards were being placed on the ground next to any and all evidence located on the ground in the area of the crime scene. One of the most significant items was an unspent .308 caliber rifle round. This changed everything when it was located. All of a sudden we were faced with the possibility that this was an armed confrontation and the decedent lost. The small amount of blood present on the body might be indicative of a small-caliber entry wound, which would provide a possible explanation for the small amount of blood present on and around the body. Also, this could explain why the action of the shotgun was in an open position and no empty shell casing was found. Perhaps the decedent was attempting to rack the shotgun and place a round in the chamber to fire at another subject armed with a rifle and the decedent lost, falling to the ground where he was shot, or maybe he managed to get off a round and the suspect picked it up in an effort to make the scene appear as a suicide rather than a homicide. At this point, anything was possible.

While detectives pondered new evidence and ran down possible leads and suspects, I received word from the detectives notifying the next of kin that the decedent's wife had positively identified him from one of the crime scene photos. This was very important because the ME's office must have a positive identification of the body, and it is not a good practice for a law enforcement officer who does not know the decedent to make the identification from a driver's license photo. This can result in liability issues and legal issues in the future long after the case is closed.

So every effort is made to have a relative, friend, coworker, or acquaintance identify the decedent.

Detectives on scene with the victim's wife also discovered that on this morning the decedent had attended the auction of their home due to foreclosure, and that the decedent had come home from the auction, left his wallet on the dresser, kissed his wife and told her that he loved her, and then left and never returned. Subsequent investigation would reveal that the decedent's wife had attempted to reach him several times that afternoon on his cell phone.

The wife provided detectives with a microcassette recorder that the decedent had used that morning to record the auction proceedings. The tape revealed that the victim had brought friends with him in an attempt to outbid potential buyers, but was unsuccessful in retaining his home. The recorder was given to detectives in order for them to review the tape and determine if the victim had left a suicide message on the recorder.

Back at the ICV, the medical examiner had checked on scene and we were about to get some answers. I crossed the crime scene tape with the ME for what seemed like the hundredth time that night and reapproached the body. An unmarked police SUV had been placed alongside the body to prevent people passing by from viewing the corpse. Unfortunately, this did not prevent the flyover of the local news channel's helicopter.

Photographs were taken of the body by the ME's office. When the ME rolled the body onto its side, blood began to pour out of three small exit wounds on the back of the victim. This was not a good indicator, but one more piece of evidence that seemed to indicate that the victim had been shot in an armed confrontation with another gunman. But it was still too early to say that for certain. The exit wounds were photographed with a scale (special ruler) to document the exit wounds' locations and sizes.

A Tyvek sheet was placed under the body and the decedent was laid on his back once again. Another sheet was held vertically to hide the body from public view, and the ME began to undress the body from neck to waist. When the ME opened the decedent's shirt, we all breathed a sigh of relief. On the subject's chest was a round entry wound that matched the diameter of the shotgun's muzzle (end of the barrel). Closer examination of the shotgun revealed a small, hardly visible sign of matter (tissue) on the muzzle. The spent shotgun shell was wedged between the chamber and ejection port. Two unspent rounds were found in the magazine of the shotgun when it was cleared for safety. This is usually done right away when a crime is still in progress, but because there was no longer a threat present and the scene was cold, the shotgun was not immediately cleared and instead preserved to maintain the integrity of the crime scene.

The ammunition found in the shotgun was Winchester Super-X nine pellet, double-ought buckshot. This would explain the small exit wounds in the victim's back. The sound witnesses heard was muffled because the decedent had taken care to place the muzzle of the shotgun under his clothing and right against his chest. He had propped the butt of the shotgun against the fence, holding the gun with his left hand by the grip of the action, using his right thumb to pull the trigger. He had leaned into the muzzle and when he fired the shot, his left hand had opened the action of the gun as he fell backward to the ground. However, this motion did not create enough force to eject the round from the chamber and ejection port of the shotgun.

The unspent .308 caliber round was determined to have been lost on the parking area of the agricultural arena following a recent gun show held at the facility. The round was not related to this incident.

An autopsy was performed at the state ME's office in the capitol, and six pellets of double-ought buckshot were recovered from the decedent's body. The manner of death was determined to be by gunshot and ruled a suicide.

It is easy to understand why the victim in this case wanted to take his life, given what must have felt like a hopeless and desperate situation to him at the time. But the sad fact of this man's demise was that he left behind a wife and several children. He was the family's sole provider and exclusive caretaker of the family's finances. By taking his own life, he selfishly abandoned his loved ones in their time of need, leaving them to not only mourn his tragic death but also to sort out their situation alone. What's more, they could not benefit from his life insurance policy because his death was by his own hand.

Based on my experience as an investigator who has attended many death scenes, suicide, with perhaps the exception of those who take their lives due to terminal illness, is always motivated by temporary circumstances and an individual's urgent desire to escape those circumstances. Sometimes you wish you could will the person to consciousness and tell them that things will get better, that help is available, that they are not alone but rather loved and cherished by someone. But like I said at the beginning of this chapter, the body of a suicide victim only speaks to us figuratively from beyond the grave, and when I arrive it's much too late for speeches and pleas. There is only time for asking what happened, picking up the pieces of a life, and trying to care for loved ones left behind, including my colleagues, which brings us full circle.

Yes, it's true, investigators make jokes and employ gallows humor about decedents and the circumstances surrounding their demise on a death scene, but it's not because we are insensitive, disrespectful, or unfeeling. Rather, it's because death is difficult and sad, even more so when surrounded by tragedy. We respond to death and destruction every day so that citizens don't have to. We are the wall and last line of defense that protects the innocence of the public and those who loved the victim.

Humor is a defense mechanism that allows us to keep going, to remain in the moment, and to undertake what seems at times like the impossible: to stand over a human corpse that is often bloody, mangled, decomposed, and sometimes not even recognizable as another human being and determine why, when, and how this person died, what killed this person, and more often than not, who killed this person. It's not an easy job, and I pray every day for the strength to do my job so you will never have to walk in my shoes.

20

BURGLARIES, THEFT, AND CRIMES OF OPPORTUNITY

As a new police officer, you're going to spend a lot of time looking at shattered car windows, homes that look like an F2 tornado ripped through their interior, or a jewelry box that *used* to hold someone's cherished family heirlooms. Burglary and theft calls are common. It just seems that some people don't understand that if something doesn't belong to them, they need to keep their hands off of it.

Most of these calls come from the victim after the crime has already occurred. Generally, they return to their vehicle from a store and find that their auto has been burglarized or return home to find the front door open and items missing from inside their residence.

Burglaries and thefts are generally crimes of opportunity, meaning the suspect viewed an item in plain sight in a car and deemed it was worth smashing a window in the vehicle to retrieve the item. In many cases, the owner of the vehicle forgot to lock their car, or just didn't even bother, assuming that it was safe in their driveway. When homes are the target, the burglar or would-be thief has probably been in the victim's home before, and knows the family's schedule and when they can be expected to be away from their residence. Sometimes the suspect is even a trusted friend of the victim or victim's family and is left alone for a few minutes in a room of the home, just long enough to grab a checkbook, iPod, cell phone, or piece of jewelry. All of these items are incredibly easy to conceal on one's person when walking out of the residence.

The responding officer will generally take a report, call for a crime scene tech to process the evidence, if any exists at the scene, and take an offense report to be forwarded to CID for follow-up investigation if the crime is a felony. Just a note here, the number one contaminator of a crime scene is a police officer. So listen up: keep your hands to yourself, watch where you step, and instruct the victim to do the same.

Crimes against property are usually graded by dollar amount, and if they are under $500, they are not assigned to CID for follow-up. In these cases, it is incumbent on the patrol officer to follow up with a misdemeanor investigation. However, the victim of this type of misdemeanor crime should request follow-up. Otherwise, it is likely that the incident will forever remain open and pending, trapped in the vacuum of "we don't have the desire or time to investigate your petty theft. Lock your doors the next time or learn to judge the character of the people you admit into your residence." Sarcastic, yes; unprofessional, yes; unfair, yes; and unacceptable, yes. Unfortunately though, this is a reality in law enforcement. So again, I would tell victims to demand the follow-up, or they can expect nothing from their police department in the case of a misdemeanor burglary or theft.

As for home invasions and robberies, these are not only crimes against property, they're crimes against persons, so you can expect an emergency response and a thorough investigation by CID.

Here's another tip: any burglary of a motor vehicle, even if the car is unlocked, is an automatic felony because the suspect/s crossed the plane of the door jamb and made unlawful entry into the vehicle. It's true even if they only took an item with a misdemeanor value. If someone breaks into a victim's residence when no one is home, but it's at an hour when someone could reasonably be expected to inhabit the dwelling, it's an automatic felony regardless of the dollar amount assigned to the stolen property. You can have a misdemeanor theft and a felony burglary.

Remember to tell victims that they need to prosecute. This is especially important when misdemeanor theft occurs. Failure to prosecute a misdemeanor crime means "no report" to the officer. No prosecution, no report. If the victim doesn't care, you don't care; that is the motto. Officers cannot prosecute a misdemeanor crime that occurs outside of their presence unless a follow-up investigation uncovers probable cause for the issuance of an arrest warrant and victims' statements are collected. Felonies are different. Law enforcement officers prosecute felonies, and it is not necessary for the felony to occur in your presence in order for you, the officer, to prosecute.

Oh, there's one more thing we need to discuss here: staged burglaries and thefts. Would someone stage a burglary or theft to conceal his or her own irresponsibility—for example, misplacing a family member's precious item or losing it altogether? Would a person stage a burglary or theft to collect insurance money when that person is down on his or her luck? Would an individual stage a burglary to cover up an aggravated robbery by a rival drug dealer, where drug money and drugs were stolen? You had better believe it! I've responded to and investigated all of these, and you will too if you decide on a career in law enforcement. Here are some things to look for when attempting to determine if a robbery or burglary has legitimately occurred or has been staged.

First, note the obvious: drawers opened, mattress overturned, items of value still in place or spread around but not damaged, items (clothes in particular) still neatly resting in the drawers that have been opened. Nothing appears riffled through. All of these are potential indicators of a staged scene. Also, consider what the so-called victims report as missing and have them include it in their written statement, if possible. If they report money missing but nothing else of value was taken, that's a problem. Or if money was taken from a less-than-obvious location that only someone familiar with the home or family would know about, that's a problem too. This can point to a robbery by a rival drug dealer. This is especially important if the victim is a known drug user or drug dealer. These are just a few things you need to consider as the responding officer. Trust me, there's more, and you'll learn what to look for and the right questions to ask over time as a patrol officer.

I don't think there's a worse feeling in this world than realizing that you have been betrayed by a close friend. Especially when that friend is someone you have been there for over the years, offering a helping hand when the person was down on his or her luck. That betrayal hurts even more when it's not just you who are betrayed by the friend's actions, but your whole family as well.

A few years ago, I was called out as a detective to investigate a home burglary in a nice, gated community in our city. The home was large and well-appointed, but not palatial enough to call a mansion. Like most homes in the area, it featured an attached garage with an outer door and large roll-up door beside it with an entrance leading from the garage into the kitchen of the residence. The house also had outer doors at the front and rear of the home.

When I arrived on scene, I made contact with the responding patrol officers and learned that the family had just returned home from a family vacation and found that the home had been burglarized. The owner of the home was the proprietor of a local car wash, and as such, he kept a safe in the house with a little extra cash for the business in the event the bank was closed or he just didn't have the time to make the deposit from the previous day of business. Missing from the safe was $20,000 in $100 bills, his Rolex watch from the dresser in the bedroom, and all the beer in the refrigerator in the garage. That was it. Nothing else in the house had been touched. Entry into the house was forced at the door leading from the garage into the kitchen, but the outer door that led into the garage had been left unlocked by the owner, which was the family's practice.

Interesting, I thought to myself. Interesting, because the family consisted of a mother, father, and two teenage daughters. The teenage daughters caught my attention when I heard about the missing beer. Not because I thought they had anything directly to do with the burglary, but because teenage girls usually attract and associate with teenage boys. And where the missing beer is concerned, just do the math. If adults over the legal drinking age of twenty-one had committed the burglary, why would they have taken the time to steal all the beer out of the fridge in the garage when they had just pocketed $20,000 in cash and a new Rolex valued at $10,000? That's a rhetorical question there. Adults of legal drinking age wouldn't have. I'll tell you why the suspects took the beer in this case. Because the burglars were adults, but not of legal drinking age; they were eighteen-year-old boys and could not purchase beer at a store, even if they had the cash for it. At least, that was my theory.

So after I had processed the scene, I interviewed the family together and learned that the homeowner, nice guy that he was, had employed a teenage boy over the last couple of years at the car wash who ended up dating one of his teenage daughters for a while, though the two were no longer together. The homeowner went on to tell me that not only had they welcomed the young man into their home when he was seeing their daughter, but that the teenage boy had also helped them move into their home and knew where the safe was because he had carried it into the house when it was installed.

"Well," said my inside voice, "imagine that." Now I think we are starting to cook on high heat here. Turns out that not only had the home-owner employed the young man, allowed him to date his teenage daughter, and gave him personal knowledge of the interior of his home and the family's patterns of coming and going, he also rode motorcycles with the young man on the weekends, as he did not have a son of his own to do that sort of thing with. He had virtually adopted the kid. I left their house that day with a name, and a pretty good idea of who the suspect was in this caper.

Sadly, the young man's name was one I knew, because I had been dealing with him as a law enforcement officer all of his teenage and young adult life. Usually he was involved in petty crimes, like stealing beer (hmmm), but if he was the suspect, this time he had crossed over the line from a misdemeanor to a serious series of felonies. Let me explain.

Burglary—entering someone's business or any other building that is not a home without the owner's consent—is a Class D felony. Entering someone's home (habitation) without consent is a Class C felony. Felonies are graded from E being the least serious to A being the worst, like first degree murder. Where a theft is concerned, the severity of the crime is determined by the amount of money or value of the property stolen. So, if you steal $500 or less in money or property, you have committed a Class A misdemeanor in addition to a Class C felony if you broke into someone's home or business to do it. If you steal over $500 in money or property but less than $1,000, it's a Class D felony theft, and so on. So the burglary charge is separate from the theft charge.

At this point in the investigation, I already knew that if I had the right suspect, he was facing one count of a Class C felony for burglary of a habitation and one count of theft over $10,000, also a Class C felony. Those are heavy charges for a young man of just nineteen, and punishable by years in the state penitentiary, not the county jail; it's the "big boy" jail. But to make matters worse, I knew the suspect's father because he was a colleague who worked for our county's sheriff's department. Yep, a cop's son was my suspect.

Through further investigation, the pieces of the story started to come together. It seems that while the family was on vacation, their teenage daughter who had been dating my suspect received a funny call from him asking if he was going to ride motorcycles with her father that weekend. The girl thought the call odd, because he, the suspect, knew that the family was already on vacation and not at home. That said, in hindsight, the call made sense. The suspect was just confirming what he already knew: that the family was out of town and away from their home.

So that weekend, the suspect and his buddy were riding around town trying to decide what they were going to do that night, and lo and behold, the suspect remembered that the family was out of town and that they kept their garage door unlocked and the refrigerator in the garage that was full of beer. I don't have to tell you what happened next, but I will.

The two young men, adults in the eyes of the law but kids to me, jumped the fence to the gated community, walked into the victim's garage, emptied the beer from the fridge into a Styrofoam cooler and started to leave, when they had another thought. Why not see if the back door to the kitchen was unlocked? It wasn't, but that didn't stop them. They forced entry, had a little look around, and then decided to jimmy the fire safe to see what was inside. They found the money and then the watch on the dresser and decided they had been there awhile and needed to split before they alarmed a neighbor.

The suspects drove to a nearby elementary school, parked in the rear of the building and split up the booty. Then they had another thought. What if they left fingerprints behind, never mind the broken door and safe and so forth. They had been watching too much *CSI* on the satellite dish. So those idiots returned to the house, pulled cleaning products from under the kitchen sink, and tried to wipe everything down they thought they may have touched in the house. I'd have laughed if I hadn't known one of the suspect's fathers and been acutely aware of the pain he was getting ready to put him through. So, now those two guys were facing not only one count of burglary, but two counts, and an additional Class C felony for tampering with evidence. These guys were just compounding their problem with every great idea that entered their heads and was acted upon.

But back to our story. The boys left the victim's home for the second time and the next morning travelled to a nearby city where they bought new motorcycles, riding gear, and with the money left over, they hit the hookah bar and smoked it up. Brilliant, right?

Well, suffice it to say that I caught up with them and got the whole story (admission) during the interview process at the police department, in writing, and on DVD. Man, was I disappointed in those young men, as were their parents, not to mention the anger and grief members of the victimized family were suffering as a result of the suspect's betrayal of their trust.

The case went to trial and the defendants, who had been caught red-handed, pled guilty and threw themselves on the mercy of the court, lamenting the fact that they were very young and that this was their first offense as adults. They even had the nerve to ask for expungement of their record once they had completed whatever sentence the judge handed down from the bench. Well, the judge was not quite so inclined to go easy on them. As it turned out, there was a sentencing enhancement that applied to the burglary charges when the offense is committed by someone who intimately knows the victim, like, I don't know, dating the victim's daughter and being a welcome member of their extended family.

The judge sentenced both young men to ten years but allowed them to serve their sentences on probation, since "this was their first offense" as adults. However, he refused expungement and told the convicted felons that they would have to live their lives with all of the consequences for employment and so on that being a convicted felon brings with it; a hard pill to swallow for a couple of nineteen-year-olds with a long life ahead of each of them. But I believe it was fair, though unfortunate and sad.

21

MOTOR VEHICLE ACCIDENTS AND DUIS

Car crashes—they're exciting and cool in NASCAR. Shards of metal slicing through the smoky air. Flaming hunks of vehicle debris tumbling thirty-five feet down the front stretch, leaving a trail of soot and smoke. The object that used to be a hood skidding across the pavement creating a tsunami of breathtaking sparks in its wake. Then everyone holds their breath as what's left of the race car finally comes to a complete, smoking stop.

The window net drops and the driver's helmet emerges through the window of the mangled debris. He looks incredulously at his beloved ride, waits for his archenemy to pass by, and throws his $1,200 form-fitted, life-saving helmet at the passing car. He is tenderly guided by race officials toward the ambulance and given a lift to the track hospital, where he is dusted off and checked for anything that needs repairing, and then he usually comes out and gives an interview, garnering valuable TV facetime for his racing team, sponsors, and adoring fans.

That's NASCAR, not public streets and interstates. The real thing that you will face every day has very different consequences.

Unless you're lucky enough to work for a police department with a dedicated traffic unit, you can plan on working property damage and injury motor vehicle accidents (MVAs) on a daily basis. You'll work them at all hours of the day and night, in all kinds of weather, on all kinds of roadways, and in every kind of traffic flow condition you can imagine.

The first rule of accident response to learn as a police officer is: "When you have inclement weather, expect accidents." Or another way of saying this might be reminiscent of the Morton Salt tagline: "When it rains, it pours." After just a few months on the job, you should be able to predict when and where accidents are going to happen by watching the weather and learning the trouble spots on the roadways in your jurisdiction. You will get to know the locations of potholes, uneven lanes, downhill grades with substandard surfaces, sharp turns, or intersections that may not be visible to the motorist in foggy conditions—all common motor vehicle hazards.

In my jurisdiction we had a "T" or "three-way" intersection where the opposite side of the intersection was a high, natural rock wall. When road conditions were foggy, a motorist unfamiliar with this intersection would not be able to see the wall on the other side of the traffic signal. If the motorist had a green light and incorrectly judged the intersection to be a four-way intersection, he or she might attempt to continue straight through the intersection at forty-five miles per hour and run right into the wall. An MVA there never surprised anyone on patrol.

Property-damage-only accidents, those in which the humans are not harmed, are generally handled with a nonemergency response. When you arrive, if motorists are okay and vehicles are moveable, you should get all concerned parties off the roadway to allow normal traffic flow to resume. If there is an injury, call for first responders and EMS personnel and go ahead and get your backup on the way. If the roadway is still open, you can anticipate its closure as soon as the fire trucks, ambulance, and tow trucks arrive on scene. So you'll need to request additional units to divert traffic onto alternate routes until you clear the accident.

We often say in law enforcement that the job is 95 percent sheer boredom and 5 percent sheer terror. Statistics vary from agency to agency, but the boring percentage makes up the vastly larger number in most jurisdictions. This definitely includes noninjury accidents. You, as a new officer, will work a lot of them, and it won't take long before you are working them by rote, almost without thinking about what you are doing. Here are a few pitfalls you should avoid, even when working a traffic accident becomes second nature.

1. Oddly enough for a police officer, it's not your job to decide who is the bad guy and who isn't, or in technical terms, determine fault in an MVA, unless you witnessed the accident as it happened. It is also most likely not within the realm of your expertise to accurately

assess a dollar amount to the damage incurred by a vehicle involved in an accident. If you are proficient at determining fault in an accident you didn't witness and then give an estimate about what it will cost to repair the vehicles, then you need to get out of law enforcement and look for a job in the auto insurance industry. You'll make a whole lot more money, have a comfortable environment to work in, and face a lot less risk and liability. Cops don't determine fault where MVAs are concerned. Attempt to, and you might as well get ready for the complaint that will follow, or in a worst case scenario, you'll have to break up a fight between the MVA parties in addition to getting the roadway back open.

2. Don't be a traffic Nazi! If the accident was clearly an accident and the result unintended, give everyone a break and forget about issuing citations. Everyone has already had a bad day, and you probably are having one too. Everyone has paid enough. Let the citation go, be the nice guy, the protector, the hero. On the other hand, if one or all of the motorists are being jerks, write them the ticket or tickets, and continue to write as long as they continue to rant. Seek out every moving violation and equipment violation you can find. Just make sure you can justify them. It's a nasty business, but it will make you feel better, and the motorist's complaint will fall on deaf ears back at the station, or in the city courtroom where the violator will be exposed for the wise guy he or she is.

3. A wise lieutenant once told me that if you give the parties involved in a noninjury accident something to do at the scene, you can keep them out of the way so you can do what you need to do. I tried it and it worked. Keep preprinted three-inch-by-five-inch index cards in your patrol unit and give them to both drivers and passengers to record their personal information, and then have them exchange cards when you wrap up. They'll be so busy writing that they won't have time to get in your way. Plus it has the added benefit of making them feel like they are helping in some way, and they are—they're staying out of your way so you can do your job.

That brings us to the injury accident. These are a different ballgame from noninjury crashes. Here, you'll be responding emergency traffic as it is likely that traffic has been interrupted and more importantly, someone is hurt and needs emergency medical attention. The fire department and EMS personnel will be dispatched before you. If you're the first officer on scene, your responsibility is to collect as much information as possible on what happened and then help divert traffic and keep motorists and pedestrians off of fire department and EMS personnel so they can render aid to the victims.

You'll also need to call for tow trucks if the vehicles cannot be moved under their own power. You don't need to worry about collecting all of your information on scene, so long as the victims are being transported to an area hospital where you can get the information later during follow-up. If the accident involves a serious injury or fatality, you'll probably have to assist with a landing zone for air evacuation by helicopter, notifications to family members, and the accident investigation if you don't have a dedicated CIRT.

Obviously, if the injury crash resulted from a criminal act like DUI, vehicular homicide, or negligent vehicular homicide, you will need to proceed accordingly. You'll probably need help, so don't be hesitant to call for backup, supervisors, and depending on the length and depth of the investigation, a mobile incident command vehicle. In this event, it's likely you'll need assistance from other city, county, or state agencies to manage the scene.

I once had a traffic officer state that I was using the wrong terminology when referring to a motor vehicle collision as an "accident." He explained that the proper term is "crash," and stated that there was no such thing as an accident. Not long after our conversation, that officer totaled his third patrol car responding to a "crash." He never received a write-up or suspension.

I happened to catch him in the break room of the police department one day. I couldn't resist asking, "Just out of curiosity, when you wrecked your third patrol car, was that an accident or a crash?" He didn't think that question was funny or clever, but he never corrected me or my terminology again. The point here is to be human, not a living badge or blind statistician. A little compassion toward your fellow man will go a long way to helping you become the public servant that citizens in your community will appreciate and admire.

When people drink an alcoholic beverage, smoke a joint, pop a pill, shoot up, or otherwise elect to alter their physical and mental state, they shouldn't get in their car and take a spin across town, or even around their front yard, for that matter.

We've all seen the public service announcements, but let me reiterate. As a police officer, sheriff's deputy, highway patrol officer, or state trooper, you will be out there on the nation's interstates, highways, city streets, back alleys, and country roads. You're a land shark, and as a new officer you should be hungry for an arrest. The drunk driver is chum in the water if they engage in the aforementioned behavior. I know I've been on the hunt for these motorists, and I have eaten my fill of chum.

As a rookie police officer, one of the most interesting, challenging, and proactive enforcement activities you can engage in is hunting for intoxicated motorists. It feels good to take someone who is a danger to himself and others off the road and into custody where the worst thing that can happen is that he wakes up in a puddle of his own urine or puke.

While the hunt for driving-impaired motorists is fun, the Field Sobriety Tasks or FSTs are often more entertaining than the foraging. It's really a lot like shooting fish in a barrel. On any given Friday or Saturday night, people will go out and cut loose. They'll drink to excess and often engage in other numbskull activities like taking ecstasy, snorting cocaine, or smoking marijuana. Other chemically impaired nut jobs will engage in sexual activity while driving down the interstate at twenty to thirty miles per hour over the posted speed limit.

Here's what you should look for as a new or veteran law enforcement officer. The first and most obvious signs of an impaired motorist are moving violations; for example:

- Speeding like the motorist is racing in the NASCAR Sprint Cup Series at Bristol Motor Speedway.
- Failure to maintain a proper lane like a Shriner on a mini-bike in your local Christmas parade.
- Failure to maintain a constant speed like your grandparents out for a Sunday drive, only it's Friday night.
- Driving in an overly cautious manner (read, "paranoid") that does not appear normal on a given stretch of roadway like, "Oh crap, I've just smoked a dime bag of weed and a cop is behind me."
- Vehicles that have equipment violations, like failure to operate headlights at night, broken lights, expired motor vehicle tags, and

excessive noise violations ranging from playing the stereo too loud to a missing or disconnected muffler.

- Occupants hanging out the windows yelling "Oink, oink" as they pass a patrol unit in traffic, or something equally clever like "I smell bacon."

Here's another easy one: window tint that exceeds the percentage of visibility authorized by the state. Usually people who tint their windows have something to hide, or at the very least think they are "too cool for school." That means they are probably arrogant enough to combine drinking and driving and attempt to get away with it.

Their lawyer on retainer is probably some goofball nicknamed something like DUI Dave with a toll-free number and a late-night television commercial that is corny as hell. Of course, there are also vehicles on the roadway operating in a dilapidated condition, motorists who forget to wear seatbelts—which in my state is a primary moving violation—and let's not forget the idiot who likes to text while driving in plain view. Remember, while it's against policy, procedure, and the law for a police officer to profile people, it's not against the law to profile vehicles.

So if a motorist is on the roadway during DUI primetime and you are out hunting, you should be trying to establish sufficient probable cause to make traffic stops in your search for DUI offenders. If you make a sufficient number of traffic stops, you'll find the DUIs.

Once you establish a reasonable suspicion that a driver has been drinking, you will administer FSTs. Drivers who don't complete the tasks to your professional standards are hauled off to jail. When drivers' blood alcohol content (BAC) comes back below the legal limit—point .08 percent in most states—they will be allowed to keep their license until the next time you catch them, but at the very least you embarrassed and inconvenienced them. Hopefully, they'll think twice before they attempt driving after they've been drinking again. Also, I should point out that even if the BAC is within the legal limit, it doesn't mean the driver wasn't impaired. Anytime you consume an intoxicating substance, your reaction time and motor skills are diminished, even if you have a high tolerance and aren't drunk according to state law. That's just scientific fact.

If a driver refuses to take the BAC test and your state has an implied consent law—a statute that requires any motorist with a driver's license in the state to submit to a blood or breath test to determine how much alcohol is in his or her bloodstream—then that driver will forfeit his or her license, even if the BAC comes back negative. Oh, and don't worry about these drivers suing you *if* you had reasonable suspicion and probable cause when you stopped them initially. You acted in "good faith." You can't help it if the results have to come back from the state before a conviction can be secured. In the meantime, you have a duty to ensure the public safety and to remove violators from the roadway.

While we're talking about DUIs, let's dispel a few other myths commonly held by the motoring public and often heard by the police officer.

- Yes, taking Sominex and six Benadryl capsules after working a sixteen-hour shift and then attempting to drive home *does* constitute impairment.
- No, your driveway is not home base where you are always safe. I can arrest you there, just like I can arrest you anywhere, when I observe you committing a crime.
- No, most people do not carry a can of Axe or Right Guard, depending on which generation you belong to, in their glove box because they think they're going to get caught in a body odor emergency.
- No, I don't keep my extra change in my vehicle in an old Crown Royal bag, and I don't buy my significant other roses from a convenience store that come in a glass cylinder bearing a striking resemblance to a crack pipe.
- And for the last time, I won't perform the FSTs with you, so don't ask.

All joking aside, DUI enforcement saves lives. It's one of the worthwhile pursuits of law enforcement, and one you should strive to perfect as a new police officer. You will lose some in court and you will win some, but don't be discouraged. You are removing dangerous drivers from the roadway while they are impaired.

Even one drink has been proven scientifically to affect motor skill function in a human being, and it doesn't matter if it's a person who's just turned twenty-one and taken his or her first drink or a career alcoholic. It affects everyone the same way in that regard.

Incidentally, if you were wondering, my best DUI arrest was a BAC of .37 at four in the afternoon on a four-lane highway, where a medical equipment delivery driver was passed out in his company van and had urinated on himself.

Dusk had just turned to darkness in our city on a stormy March night. The radio crackled to life and I was sent code 3 (lights and sirens) to a 10-46 (personal injury accident) involving a single car on a windy, rural road.

I had driven the road many times and had worked several accidents there, the last of which involved a new Ford Mustang being driven up a tree and rolled over. I arrived at that accident to find the driver hanging upside down from his seatbelt, his once-beautiful new car resting on its roof and straddling the center line. The teenager was okay, but he was in a bit of a daze. He was probably revisiting the wisdom his driver's education instructor had failed to impress upon him in the classroom lecture: "speed kills" and "don't attempt to drive beyond your ability," which at the age of sixteen is about nil.

I made it to the accident scene on the heels of the ambulance crew, who was already treating the driver in their rig. As I walked to the back of the ambulance, I observed the driver's Mercedes resting off the right side of the road, down a steep embankment and wrapped around a tree. The entire passenger side of the vehicle was crushed, to the extent that the passenger door was touching the driver's seat. Both airbags in the vehicle had been deployed, and the frame appeared to be split in half at the center.

I was about to open the back door of the ambulance when Jeff, the driver of the Mercedes, tumbled out. Jeff reeked of alcohol but didn't appear injured. I asked Jeff for his driver's license, which he said was "in his leather wallet in the car." I had Jeff sit on the bumper of my patrol car with another officer while I went to the crumpled Mercedes to get his wallet.

As I looked into the interior of Jeff's car, I found the wallet he had described, along with a box of opened wine and several pill bottles with warnings that the consumer should not "drink alcoholic beverages or operate machinery while taking this medication, as it may cause dizziness and drowsiness." Another pill bottle read, "This drug may impair the ability to drive or operate machinery." It looked as though the cause of this MVA was readily apparent, but I thought I'd ask Jeff a few questions anyway.

Jeff told me that he was currently taking the medication I observed in the passenger compartment of his Mercedes, and he admitted that he had been drinking the wine as well. Jeff said, "I'm having a bad night," and indicated that he had encountered police earlier in the evening at his residence, after having been involved in a domestic disturbance.

My sergeant had responded to the earlier call and told me that Jeff had been drinking heavily at that time and was advised to stay home and not to drive. It was evident that Jeff's consumption of alcohol and prescription medication had impaired his judgment, and that was putting it mildly.

I took Jeff through several FSTs, which he failed to execute to my satisfaction. Jeff agreed to have blood drawn to determine its alcoholic content. Jeff's blood was found to contain almost twice the legal limit of alcohol, and with that he was gone, not in sixty seconds, but with .21 grams per liter.

It came as no surprise, as I prepared for court on Jeff's case, when I discovered that he had previous convictions for driving under the influence, public intoxication, disorderly conduct, aggravated assault, possession of marijuana for resale, and driving on a revoked license. Jeff also had a warrant for his arrest out of Georgia for similar violations, but that is a story for another time.

Probably one of the most entertaining DUIs I ever worked was connected with a real-life celebrity, a country music star. No, it wasn't George Jones on a lawnmower, but it was still pretty amusing.

Just like in the case of the medical equipment van operator, it happened in broad daylight. I received a call for a 10-46, MVA with injuries, located at the base of an on-ramp to a major interstate. When I arrived on the scene, a guard rail, that ran the length of the 100-yard on-ramp, had been peeled back and coiled up like a snake getting ready to strike its prey. Past the guard rail and down an embankment rested a late-model Lincoln with severe front-end damage. On the shoulder of the road was the driver, in a tank-top, shorts, and flip-flops, sporting a mullet and a redneck Riviera-like tan. Yep, it was a country music star whose recent hit, ironically, had to do with drinking.

As soon as I made contact with him I knew he had been drinking prior to the accident. His speech was slurred, his eyes were watery and bloodshot, and he reeked of alcohol from his pores and his breath. Plus, he was unscathed, which considering the damage to his vehicle and the state's guard rail was unusual. I say unusual, but it is true. Somehow, inebriated drivers tend to stay loose instead of tensing up before an impact the way a normal, nonimpaired motorist would, so they usually avoid being hurt, thus the popular law enforcement expression, "You can't kill dirt!" Which is a way of saying bad guys, people of the lowest moral denominator, somehow have a way of coming out better than the victim.

But, I digress. Once my backup arrived, I started going over FSTs with the suspect, who had initially agreed to cooperate and perform said tasks. While I was explaining and demonstrating the one-leg stand, the suspect kept tapping me on the elbow and suggesting that I "do the tasks with him." I kept my cool and brushed this off the first time, but the second time he tapped me on the elbow with his suggestion, I informed him that he could either keeps his hands to himself and follow my instructions, or I would just go forward under the assumption that he did not wish to perform the tasks. That is to say, "take him to jail for DUI." You don't want to use those words though, because if you do, you are forecasting to the suspect what you intend to do and giving him a chance to resist. That said, even my innocuous statement was enough for this guy. In the time it takes to snap your fingers, his whole demeanor changed right there on the roadside. He stopped smiling, balled his fists at his side, and right then and there declared that I was something not fit to print. He followed that statement with a swing in my direction, but I anticipated it because of the balling of his fists, a nonverbal signal to the officer that a punch is about to be thrown. I caught his wrist mid-swing and spun him around, placing his fist in the small of his back, while my backup officer grabbed his other arm. The suspect was summarily "cuffed and stuffed," as they say on television. Several months later, the suspect appeared in circuit court and pled guilty to DUI. I could have charged him with assault, but sometimes you just let things go. We refer to that as "officer discretion." Sure, technically he assaulted me just by calling me a bad word and following it up with a swing in my direction, even though he didn't connect. But no harm, no foul. I was none the worse for the wear, and frankly, that wasn't the worst thing I had ever been called in the course of performing my duty as a law enforcement officer, and it certainly would not be the last time I would be cussed at. If you do not have thick skin and tend to wear your heart on your sleeve, you won't be a cop for long, I can assure you.

22

DRUGS, NARCOTICS, AND A CESSPOOL OF MISERY

I wear my sunglasses at night. Not just a song, it's a way of life for crack heads who haven't sold the sunglasses off their face yet. Cool factor aside, the sunglasses hide their pinpoint pupils, which should be open wide at night to allow in enough light to see. Stimulants cause pupils to constrict at night when they should be dilated to allow more light in to aid sight, while depressants cause pupils to dilate, which during the day keeps the pupil open when it should be constricted to block sunlight; these are clues that help officers determine what class of drug someone is under the influence of. Of course, if you are smoking a lot of weed and your pupils are dilated wide during the day, you'll want to wear your sunglasses to block out the excruciating pain that the excessive light causes. Alcohol does this too. That's why sunglasses are popular the day after a heavy night of drinking, when someone is hungover.

One night while enjoying a quick bite at a local diner, another officer and I observed a vehicle pull up outside of the restaurant. A college kid got out with his girlfriend, and without hesitating, walked right into the diner's plate glass door, bounced off, stumbled backward, and fell on his rear end in the parking lot next to his car. Now let's face it. This is not normal behavior, even for someone who is distracted by a cell phone call or just deep in thought. Trust me, the diner's window wasn't clean enough so as to appear nonexistent.

My partner and I walked outside. While my partner sat the guy upright and attempted to engage in conversation with him, I took a stroll around the car to peer into the interior. In plain view were used (punctured) CO_2 cartridges commonly used in B.B. guns and whipped cream cans to propel a projectile or food product. These are also referred to by their illicit name as "whippets." They're called whippets because of their use in conjunction with whipped cream. The user puts one end of the cartridge in the opening of a balloon and punctures the cartridge, causing the CO_2 to be released into the balloon. The user then inhales the contents of the balloon, becoming lightheaded and dizzy. Often this inhalant is used in conjunction with other drugs; in this case, Valium, marijuana, and alcohol, all central nervous system (or CNS) depressants.

We were legally able to search the car and discover the other drugs because the CO_2 cartridges were in plain view in the back floorboard of the vehicle. That, coupled with the driver's behavior, gave us the reasonable suspicion and/or probable cause to believe that the driver was using the CO_2 for an illicit purpose and that other drugs were likely present in the vehicle.

The funny thing is, we never would have left our cheeseburgers if the driver had not unintentionally given himself away by traveling around in public while under the influence of a combination of legal and illegal substances.

Glorified by television and gangster rap, drugs and narcotics are still an illegal but viable way for many individuals to earn a living. Though the market has changed over the years, the popular drugs have new names, and many of them come from a medicine cabinet or prescription bottle, the wholesale violence that results from their sale remains the same. The violence ebbs and flows with the popularity of different prescription and illicit drugs, their side effects, and their availability. However, the violence that stems from the drug-selling trade is always there.

Talk to any officer who patrols a drug-infested area of their jurisdiction and they'll say the same. Where there are drugs being sold and consumed, there will be violence and unpredictable behavior. It's an uphill battle, one we are not likely to win, and one that eats law enforcement resources and takes our attention away from other problems in the city that desperately need to be addressed.

Every young officer wants to make drug arrests, and you will be no different. Here are a few things you need to know.

In most communities, the players will remain the same over the years until they are removed from the street and put in prison, die, or are killed.

Then someone else in the culture will step up to take over their business where they left off. Some of the activity they engage is in tied into gang activity, but a lot of it is just plain commerce.

If you, as a junior officer, don't have the confidence to patrol the low-income and public housing areas of your community, then you will have a much harder time finding drugs and locating sellers. It's important for officers to get into the community where the dealing is going on and to cultivate relationships with community members in the know.

Citizens willing to help the police exist in every community and they will talk to you, but it won't happen overnight. If you are a minority officer, you may have an advantage, but even then you will have to work at building your sources. This means making contacts by shaking down street-level dealers and their buyers and being willing to cut minor offenders a break in return for their cooperation down the road when their information really matters.

Like all police work, you'll need to keep your eyes and ears open. You'll need to watch for hand-to-hand transactions that occur in the open on street corners. Look for cars that don't fit into the demographic of the neighborhood and continually turn blocks (drive in circles around the block over and over again). Search for drivers who pick up people standing on the corner and then return them to the same corner a few minutes later. Also, look for out-of-state license plates in the neighborhood from faraway places like Alaska, for instance. This is likely a stolen car, plate, or dealer from out of town. Plus, don't forget to seek out the all-important and obvious advertisement of the old tennis shoes hung over a telephone wire, indicating that drugs are sold at that location.

Armed with these techniques, a list of important contacts, the cooperation of the prominent and respected members of the community, and a lot of luck, you'll make a dent in the drug and narcotic dealing in your jurisdiction.

Today the common drugs you'll find on the street include crack cocaine; marijuana; methamphetamine; ecstasy, also known as methylenedioxymethamphetamine (MDMA); heroin; peyote buttons (mescaline); psilocybin (mushrooms); khat (Catha edulis); synthetics like bath salts and air fresheners; inhalants like toluene and nitrous oxide; alkyl nitrates like Rush; cough suppressants like syrups that contain DXM (dextromethorphan); and prescription medications like ketamine (Special K), Lortab, OxyContin, oxycodone, Xanax, Adderall, Ritalin, and sleeping pills like Ambien.

You'll also find vials of morphine, Demerol, powder cocaine, or maybe even GHB, a liquid date rape drug that looks like water but bubbles when shook up like liquid dish soap, but it's an extremely rare day when you luck up on hashish or LSD on blotter paper. However, while some of these drugs have been out of vogue and their delivery mechanisms are antiquated, they are making a comeback as prescription opioids and synthetic equivalents are becoming harder to get. They are still present in some form or variety in large, urban areas. Also, keep an eye out for counterfeit pills that look like prescription narcotics, but are likely to contain dangerous, very powerful drugs, like fentanyl. Just three grains, like sand, of this drug will kill the user. It's fifty times more potent than heroin and one hundred times more potent than morphine.

Drugs move, so you can often find them by making traffic stops along their known paths of travel, and a lot of foot traffic in a community is a sure sign that drugs are around. Get out of the car, walk foot paths, and engage in numerous traffic stops in these areas, and you will find the drugs. Just make sure you do it with a partner nearby or with you.

People who use drugs are easy to spot when you know what their typical habits and behaviors look like. Drug users and dealers don't usually move around in the daytime, though this is changing as street-level narcotics officers focus more on nighttime operations. Still, you'll generally want to work evening or midnight shift to be up when the dealers and buyers are out and about. Look for obvious signs, like someone standing on the same corner for an extended period of time and getting in and out of different vehicles at the same location. When you are speaking to someone on the street, look for signs like erratic behavior, needle tracks, body sores, nervous tics, and less obvious signs like dilated eyes in the daytime and contracted pupils at night, or "pinpoints" as officers like to refer to them. All these things will help you identify the users.

The dealers are also fairly easy to identify at the street level. They'll always be working corners or standing in vacant lots and in front of known drug houses, but don't expect them to have the drugs on their person. Those days are long gone. They'll send for the drugs or go get them after they make arrangements with the buyer. So expect more than one interaction between the customer and the seller before the drugs show up. When they do arrive, the deal goes down fast, so be ready to enter the ball game and be prepared to articulate your reasonable suspicion or probable cause in your arrest warrant.

If you are lucky and you work at it, you'll get some drugs off of the street and shut down a few dealers, interrupting the network for a while, but know that there is always someone ready to take the place of the previous dealer. The business will survive your enforcement action, so count on repeating the aforementioned steps over and over again.

Many junior officers find this kind of work exciting, but it takes a lot of patience for a little action. At the end of the day, there's a lot of paperwork and court time to follow. Don't be surprised if you find yourself getting bored and wanting to return to the more traditional aspects of policing. It's called burnout, and it's normal. The more you rotate around in your career as a law enforcement officer and the more you try different jobs within the department, the more likely you'll be to remain fresh, interested, and up-to-date.

We've all watched *COPS* and heard tell of the stupid criminal. Even so, criminals still keep on committing offenses and demonstrating their lack of acumen, or brain cells for that matter. The two Einsteins I met one night as I was preparing to head home from shift were no exception.

I had just finished a 3 p.m. to 1 a.m. tour and had parked my patrol car at a local convenience store at the edge of our city. We had take-home cars, but those of us who lived in neighboring counties still had to drive our personal vehicles to and from work. I was gassing up my truck for the ride home when a beat-up blue sedan occupied by two white males pulled into the parking lot of the store but stopped short of the parking stalls when they saw me at the fuel pumps. I was still in uniform.

As we made eye contact, the two guys in the car ducked down in their seats behind the dashboard as if they were hiding something. Their behavior was odd, if not outright suspicious, to say the least. I continued to fuel my POV and watch as the guys in the sedan emerged from their slouched position and continued in the car toward a parking stall.

Interestingly enough, before they pulled all the way in, they stopped again. The driver looked back over his shoulder at me for the second time. Hey, I may not be a rocket scientist, but even I knew that these guys needed some attention from law enforcement.

Finally, they pulled into the parking stall, but neither of them exited the vehicle. That's strange if you think about it. How many times have you seen a car pull up to a convenience store with two occupants inside and no one gets out? Never, right?

I finished topping off my tank of gas and returned the nozzle to the gas pump, starting my approach to the vehicle. I was still wearing my duty gear, so I turned on my portable radio and called out my location and activity to dispatch. It was summertime and even though it was dark outside, it was still warm. The windows on the beat-up sedan were down, and I knocked on the door post of the car to alert the driver to my presence.

I identified myself and asked the guys what they were up to. The driver, who was busy messing with something in the center console, didn't even acknowledge my presence. I announced myself a second time, which seemed to startle the driver, who turned around in his seat revealing a small, metal rod with a burnt end (tamping rod) in his left hand. A tamping rod is used to push a crack cocaine rock or crystal meth into a glass pipe or tube for smoking. As the driver shifted in his seat, the glass crack pipe rolled out from under his leg, complete with wire screen used for a filter.

I ordered the passenger to put his hands on the dashboard where I could see them and ordered the driver out of the vehicle, cuffing him as soon as he emerged and sitting him down on the edge of the store's sidewalk. I radioed for backup, and when it arrived, I searched the driver and found crack cocaine, powdered cocaine, and marijuana all packaged for resale. While I was waiting for another unit to arrive, I noticed that the driver's side interior door panel was missing and that a butcher knife was stuck in the door. Additionally, the column on the beat-up sedan was punched, and sure enough, it was stolen.

This was starting to look like the Holy Grail of investigatory stops, and the hits just kept coming. As it turned out, the guy in the passenger seat was a juvenile who had run away from state's custody in a neighboring jurisdiction and had hooked up with the male driver of the car at a crack house. The teenager agreed to exchange sex with the man for drugs. What's more, they had both been using, so the driver was charged with DUI in addition to felony possession of a stolen vehicle, felony possession of a Schedule Two and Schedule Four narcotic for resale, possession of an illegal weapon, and contributing to the delinquency of a minor.

Needless to say, my already long shift had just gotten longer. I didn't mind, though; it's what we (law enforcement officers) do, and it served as just another reminder that "Stupid Is as Stupid Does."

"Which one of these kids is doing his own thing?" That's a question I liked to ask myself regularly when I was working gang and street-level drug enforcement in our city. One particular night, just before dark, my partner and I rolled into a cul-de-sac at the end of a short street. Back up against the curb at the end of the street, and technically in the street, was a white, late-model Cadillac with low-profile tires and big rims occupied by three male subjects. It was a summer evening, and all the windows of the car were down. As we pulled up and exited our unmarked vehicle, a Jeep Grand Cherokee with tinted windows, I could immediately smell burning marijuana coming from inside the vehicle—and no, burning marijuana doesn't smell like burning rope, it smells like burning marijuana. As a new officer, you'll be exposed to controlled burns so you can recognize and testify to the smell.

When I reached the driver's side door, the driver of the vehicle was holding a burning blunt, and I observed white powder lined out across the dash of the car. The driver, to his credit, immediately admitted to smoking a blunt sprinkled with cocaine, or what's known in street terminology as a "heavy," so I asked him to step out of the vehicle, cuffed him, and searched his person. Not shockingly, I came across the equivalent of about half a pound of individually packaged "nugs" of marijuana—that's urban parlance for bud in nuggets of varying sizes and quality. So it was pretty obvious this guy was dealing in addition to consuming. All of the occupants were under the age of twenty-one and there was open alcohol in the car, so everyone was taken out of the vehicle. My partner noticed that the backseat passenger was standing kind of crooked, putting all of his weight on one foot, so we had him kick off his shoes, and what did we find? Surprise, surprise, fourteen grams of powder cocaine, from whence the dashboard coke came. Not only did we arrest all of the occupants and take them to jail, but we also seized and later sold the Cadillac at auction with the proceeds going to the department's drug fund.

The sad part of the story is that the backseat passenger with the coke was on a full-ride basketball scholarship to a local university, and now he had blown it, no pun intended. What's more, the coke he was supposed to be dealing, not using, was fronted to him, meaning he had not paid for it.

Now the police had it. So he would have to pay back the dealer or, well, let's just say, it's likely the debt would be collected one way or another, and neither way is preferable for the guy who lost the dope.

23

SHOPLIFTING, OR FIVE-FINGER DISCOUNTS

If you work in a jurisdiction where you have a mall, a strip mall, or any retail area, you will be arresting shoplifters, usually after having received a dispatch to respond to a store where a loss prevention (LP) officer has a shoplifter detained.

These are easy jobs because the LP has already done the work for you. The LP is likely to have a video of the incident, will have witnessed the shoplifter secret the item or items on his or her person, and observed the shoplifter pass all points of purchase without paying. You'll take a report, the LP will sign the warrant, and you'll transport the shoplifter to jail.

I suppose this is as good a time as any to mention that all crimes are accompanied by one or more elements that you could identify as the suspect's motive or motives, and shoplifting is no exception.

The three primary motives are drugs, sex, and money. Drug addicts need money to "re-up" (buy more drugs or resupply) and cannot maintain gainful employment due to their drug use. So they often shoplift to sell items for cash to buy drugs, or trade the items to the dealer for drugs. Some people steal because they are down on their luck and cannot stand to lose their standard of living.

Kids often steal for the kick or because mom and dad won't buy them something they want or think they are entitled to have. Sometimes people steal to provide items to a girlfriend or boyfriend to keep them happy and sufficiently impressed so they can get sex. Those are just a few of the reasons people steal and otherwise commit crime, but again, you'll find one or more in every crime to which you respond.

There are seasons prone to increased shoplifting, like Christmas, Valentine's Day, and back to school, so expect increased activity around those dates. You'll also get more shoplifting calls if your retail area is near a major thoroughfare or interstate, where there is more than one avenue of escape that can be accessed quickly by the thief.

Areas where it's easy to get lost in a crowd or traffic also provide a good cover for the shoplifter's escape. We had all of those elements in one place in the jurisdiction where I worked as an officer, so trying to find a vehicle described as a white sport utility vehicle leaving the scene was like trying to spot a needle in a haystack of needles, meaning every soccer mom was driving a vehicle that could be described that way. There were a blue million of them on the road. I could spit and hit one matching that description. So details were very important to me when trying to apprehend a shoplifter who had fled in a vehicle.

Speaking of vehicles, you will need to try to get access to the vehicle the shoplifter arrived in. Ask the shoplifter for consent to search his or her vehicle or if there is any merchandise in the vehicle that is stolen. Another approach is to find out where it's parked and just take a walk around the vehicle. If you can identify stolen items in plain view or evidence of stolen items being in the car—for example, removed price tags in the floorboard of the car with scissors—you will be able to build your reasonable suspicion, and in no time it will become probable cause. Chances are you'll identify other stores that the shoplifter has already hit. Shoplifters often work in teams, so try to get them to identify their partners and any vehicle involved. You can do this by reviewing their cell phones' incoming and outgoing calls and text messages and reviewing the store's surveillance tape, or just ask the shoplifters in custody. They'll rat out their associate if there is possibly something in it for them. There doesn't have to be in reality. The officer just implies it in conversation and allows the shoplifters to draw their own conclusion. If it's the wrong one, that is not the officer's problem. After all, we all know the saying about making assumptions.

Finally, and especially during the holidays, keep an eye on your fire lanes, where shoplifting teams often park in order to run to the nearest clothing rack, grab an armful of expensive merchandise, and make a quick getaway. Actively enforce your fire lanes during this time and keep them empty. You'll prevent a lot of shoplifting and catch a lot of shoplifters. You'll probably score some illegal drugs and their owners, too.

In previous paragraphs, we discussed that one of the motivations for shoplifting was to obtain money for the next fix, meaning more drugs. This is that kind of tale.

When I was dispatched to one of our anchor stores at the mall to a shoplifting in progress, I wasn't exactly sure what to expect. I had a description of the suspect's vehicle, and I knew that it was in the parking lot of the store and occupied by one female while two male suspects were actively shoplifting in the store. The LP officers had provided the communications officer with that detail. However, I cannot honestly say I anticipated what I would find when I arrived on scene.

The plan, coordinated while I was on the way with the store's LP officers, was for me to make contact with the woman in the vehicle. Then, with her in custody and on the way to jail with another unit, I would come inside and take custody of the male suspects. This, of course, was contingent on them having been detained by store personnel. By the time I arrived, the men had already made a trip to their minivan to deposit the circular saws they had initially lifted from the tool department of the store.

I pulled up near the minivan and made contact with the female occupant, asking her to step out of the vehicle in the event that she had access to a weapon in the minivan. After I had frisked her for my safety, I asked her to tell me what was going on, giving her a taste of what I already knew to encourage her to tell the truth rather than feed me some bullshit story.

I could tell from looking at her eyes that she was under the influence of a depressant because her pupils were dilated and it was a bright sunshiny day outside. Normally when it's sunny outside, your pupils close because your eyes are trying to optimize for the increased light and shut out the glare. Just the opposite is true at nighttime. If an individual's pupils are small (pinpoints) in the dark, that lets an officer know that a stimulant is on board because they should be open to let in more light due to the darkness.

Not surprisingly, she gave me a ridiculous story about what her and her companions were doing at the mall. I asked her if I could take a look in the vehicle and she gave me consent to search, which she probably would not have done under normal circumstances, but again, she was high and not exercising sound judgement. Before searching the vehicle, I asked her the usual, "Is there anything in the van that might poke me or stick me, or harm me in some way?" to which she replied "Yes." So I inquired as to what that was and where it was.

The female suspect told me that one of the men with her was a diabetic and that he had his diabetic pouch in the vehicle. Expecting illicit IV drug use, I asked her to obtain it for me. She did, and when I unzipped the pouch, thirty used needles spilled out onto the pavement of the parking lot, along with a spoon with drug residue and a tourniquet. Now, I'm not a medical professional, but my father is a type 2 diabetic who has to inject insulin. And anyone who knows a diabetic of this kind or has one in their family knows that when a diabetic injects insulin, they do it subcutaneously, which is to say that they insert the needle into the fatty tissue just below the surface of the skin, not in the vein where illicit drug users inject narcotics, tying the arm off with a tourniquet. Plus, my dad's procedure doesn't require heating up insulin in a coffee spoon.

I related that information to the female and asked her politely if she didn't want to "start over from the beginning" of her story and this time tell me the truth? Deducing, even in her state of mind, that the jig was up, she told me the whole story. Here's how it goes.

The woman and the two men were from a nearby metropolitan city and had only a few hours before scored (purchased illegally) several pills of a prescription medication and controlled substance (powerful narcotic) called OxyContin. Oxy is an opioid pain medication that is not unlike Demerol, morphine, or their illicit cousin heroin. Being avid drug users and short on cash, the three suspects immediately heated up and injected the Oxy as soon as they purchased it to stave off withdrawal symptoms, then drove their van to our city to steal power tools to pawn in the metropolitan area for quick cash to buy more Oxy. Well, now this story made more sense.

As soon as my backup unit arrived and the female suspect was on her way to jail, I made contact with the LP officers in the store and took custody of the male suspects, who confirmed their associate's story.

However, like most of these calls, there was a twist. It seems that the pawnshop owner where the suspects were going to unload the circular saws would not take them without blades, so that's why the men went back into the store for a second time and ultimately got caught. And guess where they were secreting the saw blades with carbide tips (making them extremely hard and sharp)? Yep, down the front of their pants. I couldn't help but chuckle on the way to the jail with the men, thinking about what might have happened had they decided to try to run from an LP officer and fell with those saw blades down the front of their pants. Not the wisest move, but then neither is drug abuse or shoplifting.

Shoplifting is graded (misdemeanor/felony) just like theft, according to the dollar amount stolen. Shoplifting, like burglaries, is also often a crime of opportunity, but unlike burglary, shoplifting usually takes place in plain view of the general public in a retail setting, and the motives vary from suspect to suspect. Some perpetrators of this crime are part of shoplifting rings that travel from location to location and state to state to avoid getting nabbed. Others are executed by one or two individuals who want to trade or exchange merchandise for cash or drugs. The merchandise is often fenced through a legitimate retail outlet and sold at half its normal face value. These underhanded merchants range from local discount and clearance warehouses, to street and flea market vendors, to dirty pawnshop owners, and even to criminals selling stolen merchandise out of the trunk of a car in the box store parking lot. The merchandise, once stolen, can often be hard to identify in terms of its origin, as identifiers are often removed or obscured by the thieves or criminal fences. These items are often purchased knowingly by consumers who just don't care where their bargain came from. But buyer beware: if you are caught with stolen merchandise, you will have to forfeit it along with the money you proffered when you purchased stolen merchandise, whether you were aware that it was hot or not. The moral of the story is if the deal seems too good to be true, it probably is.

I got a call for service once for two guys that were shoplifting video games at a gaming chain store. When I made contact with them, they had bags of stolen games still in the packaging. Further investigation of their vehicle in the parking lot of the strip mall revealed empty digital video disk (DVD) security boxes, wrappers, and scissors—all of these in plain view on the floorboards of the car. Those guys were serial shoplifters, but as a police officer, you'll also have to deal with folks shoplifting food at the grocery store, stealing over-the-counter medications for illicit drug manufacturing, teenage girls stealing clothing that mom and dad will not buy them or allow them to purchase, teenage boys stealing the latest electronics for their cars, and more.

Some of these cases are just sad and emanate from a place of economic disadvantage and plain poverty. The really unfortunate nature of these types of shoplifting events is that if the people down on their luck would only put their pride aside and seek help from their community, nine times out of ten, churches, community organizations, foodbanks, and so on are there waiting and willing to help with food, clothing, personal care items, over-the-counter medications, and shelter.

In my jurisdiction, not only did we have community-sponsored programs to help folks down on their luck, we had forms, contact numbers, and transportation at the ready to assist anyone who asked for help with these problems. I, and most officers I worked with, were only too happy to facilitate contact for people who asked and make sure that they were taken care of. It was one of the pleasures of my job. I hope it will be one of yours too, should you decide to pursue a career in law enforcement.

24

CRITICAL INCIDENTS AND THE USE OF DEADLY FORCE

When the term "critical incident" is batted around in law enforcement, it's usually being used to describe enforcement actions that require the use of deadly force. Maybe an officer shot someone or was shot by a suspect. Maybe the event resulted in a loss of life. Regardless, it's almost always tied to the use of deadly force or threatened use of deadly force by an officer, officers, or the suspect.

There are certain times as a police officer when you will be faced with the prospect of using deadly force. You'll train for these scenarios and be able to identify them without even thinking about them, which is how it should be. When these events occur, you will not have time to think about what you are going to do; you'll just react to the threat in front of you (fall back on your training), hopefully. If you don't react, you'll probably end up on the medical examiner's slab, which is not the place you want to be.

Deadly force is always the last resort. You should not want to use it or even be in a situation to use it if there is any possible way to avoid it. However, there are certain situations that require its employment. The first we'll look at is the edged-weapon attack.

Any time you encounter a knife in the hands of a suspect, you should know that on average the suspect can close the distance between you and the blade of that knife in a matter of one or two seconds if they are within your twenty-one-foot safe zone. Count that off right now. One. Two.

That is a short amount of time, isn't it? In those two seconds, you will need to recognize the threat, assess the potential danger to you, determine if the suspect is approaching you to harm you, determine exactly how the suspect intends to attack you (thrust, slice, upper body, chest, face, throwing the weapon, etc.), plan your defensive or offensive maneuver, and then execute that maneuver. In two seconds.

That's when training kicks in. If you are properly trained and stay on top of your game, you don't have to go through all of those steps, you'll just instantly act, saving you valuable and possibly life-saving time.

But, as with most dangerous actions, the best way to avoid getting hurt or hurting someone is to avoid being put in a position where that can happen.

Your body armor won't stop an edged-weapon attack, and if the person is already on the move, you won't have your gun out of the holster. It's too late. If you encounter a knife, you need to address it immediately with a drawn service weapon and commands to the suspect. Order the suspect to put the knife down! If the suspect starts to close on you, you need to drop that person like a hot rock! I'm serious here.

Anytime a gun is in play, it's the same thing. You're going to have to meet it with the threat of deadly force being applied. Ideally, you'll have a less-lethal option, like an officer with a bean bag round or Taser, to improve the odds that you won't have to shoot the suspect. Nevertheless, you will have to be prepared to pull the trigger if the suspect is threatening your life, the life of an innocent civilian, or the lives of your fellow officers.

You will encounter individuals who are emotionally distraught and threaten to kill themselves with a knife or a gun, when what they really want is for you to end their life for them. This is commonly referred to as the "suicide-by-cop" scenario. Believe it or not, it shouldn't affect how you respond. Again, if a gun or knife is present, all bets are off. No officer wants to assist someone in committing suicide, but at the end of the day, if it's going to be you or them, it needs to be them. Don't second-guess yourself because seconds count.

Deadly force is also an equalizing option. If you are a small officer, then you can rely more on the tools that hang on your duty belt rather than engage in hand-to-hand combat. A small officer, when facing a large suspect, may be able to justify the employment of deadly force against the offender if, for instance, you are being choked out and are likely to lose consciousness. After all, you are carrying a gun, and if you lose consciousness while being choked out by the suspect, you will lose control of the firearm. That means the potential exists that you could be killed with your own gun.

In that case, you may be able to shoot the suspect, even though they are not armed with a knife or a gun. Just make sure you can articulate why you did what you did. Then be prepared to rely on the common sense and goodness of the members of your local community who will make up a jury that will decide whether or not you acted appropriately. Always remember: "It's better to be tried by twelve than to be carried by six!"

It's not an ideal situation and a pretty uncomfortable one, but it's a scenario you should be prepared for if you want to do this job. We often say that the officer has only seconds to make a decision that could affect the life and death of everyone concerned, but the jury has as much time as it wants to assess that decision. This is also referred to as "Monday morning quarterbacking," that is, "If I had been that officer, I would have (fill in the blank)." Police officers hate that, but it's a fact you'd better get used to.

Following every critical incident, you can expect to be asked to make an initial statement and then attend a critical incident stress debrief. The debrief will last for a few hours and may not take place until a day or two has elapsed from the time of the incident. Your department will likely have a counselor or psychologist/psychiatrist already on call to conduct the stress debrief. They will work with you to assess your feelings, emotions, and mental well-being in the wake of your use of deadly force.

Remember, these people are there to help you, and you need to let them. It's not the time to be tough or push stuff down, because trust me, it will come up later when you least expect it. The incident does have the potential to affect you physically and mentally if you don't address it on the front end. Taking a life is a terrible thing and difficult at best for the officer, even if the officer's actions were justified.

You'll be placed on administrative leave pending the outcome of the official investigation, usually conducted by a state law enforcement agency or bureau of investigation. An internal investigation into your actions will be conducted by the department, and you are obligated to cooperate or be subjected to possible termination.

When it comes time to make your official statement in the criminal investigation, be sure you have your lawyer present for any and all questioning about the incident. You won't offend your supervisors or the department, as they will expect that and will probably even give you time to get your ducks in a row.

Some officers, particularly those who are exposed to critical incidents frequently due to the nature of the jurisdictions they work in, will develop PTSD as a result of their exposure. Their figurative accelerator will be stuck in the full-throttle position, causing the constant release of powerful chemicals like adrenaline and cortisol into their bodies. This triggers the fight-or-flight response, and as a police officer, I don't have to tell you which one you'll choose.

This will cause problems at home, but can also create real and very significant problems on the job where an officer is constantly provoked, and it's necessary to keep emotions and reactions in check. Just remember that having PTSD does not mean you're crazy. It's just a psychological reaction to a physiological problem.

It can generally be addressed with counseling and antidepressant medication. Know that you are not alone. Many officers suffer from this condition and function fine at home and on the job if they get the help they need. Unfortunately, many self-medicate with alcohol and drugs, and some even become abusers or overly aggressive officers on the street. This often causes them to start escalating situations, and even create situations that at the very least result in complaints and at their worst result in injury or the loss of career and family. Get help. It's out there, and you are worth it.

25

SPECIALTIES IN LAW ENFORCEMENT

One of the great things about pursuing a career in policing is that everyone starts at the bottom as a patrol officer and learns the basics. There is so much to know and learn working the street, and you will not experience and master it overnight. But, usually, at about the five-year point, an officer has built a solid foundation in terms of his acumen and ability to handle most situations effectively on patrol. So to keep up a high level of employee engagement and to keep the officer from becoming bored or complacent and seeking another job, most departments, if they have the budgetary means, will encourage the officer to specialize in an area of interest, seek promotion, or both.

There are many disciplines to choose from as a seasoned officer, and while this is by no means a comprehensive list, it's a good sampling of the possibilities. Some of the options may include:

- SWAT (Special Weapons and Tactics)
- K-9 (Police Dog Handler)
- Dive Team (Underwater Searches and Recovery)
- Traffic Enforcement (Accident Investigations/Directing Traffic/ DUI Enforcement/Child Safety Seat Installations/Active Enforcement to Prevent Accidents from Occurring)
- Bike Unit, Flex (Plain Clothes Street Crime and Gang Enforcement)
- FTO (Training New Police Recruits)
- Air Unit (Police Aviation)

- Patrol Sergeant (Supervision of First Line Officers)
- Crime Scene Technician (Crime Scene Processing)
- Detective Division or CID (Criminal Investigations usually broken down into specialized units consisting of detectives who investigate: Major Crimes, Special Victims, Vice/Narcotics, and Internet Crimes Against Children)

Also available are special assignments like protecting dignitaries, inter-agency assignment to a task force of the FBI, US Marshall's Service, ATF, or even the DEA. And, of course, if you have the stomach for it, Internal Affairs (investigating other officers).

Whatever you choose, you'll likely be around for at least twenty-five years before you are eligible to retire and draw a full pension, so choose wisely and know that you have time to try several different avenues if you can remain in good standing with your agency and don't make too many political waves in your department.

I chose to compete for and then accept a promotion to detective within my agency at the five-year mark. I was assigned to the Major Crimes Unit that works any felony crime related to property or any violent felony where the parties involved do not know each other or do not have a domestic relationship—those fall to the Special Victims Unit, popularly referred to on television as the SVU.

During my first five years, I prepared for my move to CID by demonstrating interest and initiative in the discipline, working misdemeanor investigations, processing crime scenes as a crime scene tech, and serving as an FTO training new police officers. So when it came time to test, my colleagues in CID knew who I was, my work ethic, and my desire to learn. That made all the difference and made me more than just a good test score when they were considering me to join their team.

If you are fortunate enough to be selected for a specialized unit, you'll likely have to attend additional schools to train in your new specialty. For example, as a new detective I attended a school for criminal investigations, and traveled to the St. Louis University School of Medicine, where I attended and completed the Medicolegal Death Investigation training course. These types of specialty schools are tough, and you must succeed if you want to pursue the specialty you've been selected for. In my career, I've also attended Patrol Response to Street Level Drugs at the Regional Counterdrug Training Academy, Interview and Interrogation with the

Reid School, Field Training Officer's school, bike school, and many more. As a general rule, you should try to attend at least one specialized school relative to your job every year. These schools can be expensive and if you come from a small department I would encourage you to look for local, free, or inexpensive schools sponsored by departments and universities near you. It's hard for supervisors to say no to free.

Later, I would return to patrol and end my career working in plain-clothes as a Flex officer assigned to street crimes and gang enforcement. But, enough about all that. Here's another good detective story. Enjoy.

I stood over the body of the middle-aged man and stared down at the hole on the left side of his nose, just below the bridge where a person's glasses might rest. I didn't need any special forensic training to deduce what had happened to him. I already knew the backstory. Hours earlier, a clerk had found the body of the male victim's fiancée in the front passenger seat of her car, parked behind the neighborhood convenience store nearest her home. She was in an uncomfortable position, with three bullet holes in her torso. Preliminary investigation would reveal a record of several calls for police service to her residence to take down complaints of harassment against her and her new fiancé by a jealous ex-lover. Anyone could have put the pieces together to solve the puzzle of the suspect's identity.

No, it wasn't the investigation that held interest for me on this, my first callout as a detective with the city police department. Rather, it was the up-close-and-personal brush with the thought of my own mortality and the sudden demise of the couple.

Why, just that morning the female victim found in the vehicle behind the local Rippy Mart had been getting ready for work in her bathroom, applying makeup to her face in the predawn incandescent lighting before her ex arrived unannounced. He shot her new fiancé on entry and literally pulled her from her morning routine. That was evident from the mascara tube and eye-lining pencil located between the victim's bathroom and the back door leading from the kitchen, where her fiancé lay lifeless, in front of the door leading to the garage.

The suspect had shot the male victim at close range with a revolver, as one could surmise from the conspicuous lack of bullet casings on the floor where they would have been obvious had the suspect used a semi-automatic handgun. Casings remain in the wheel of a revolver once fired until they are manually ejected by the gunman, while casings from a semiautomatic handgun are automatically ejected from the firearm when its action cycles after discharge, leaving them strewn on the ground. Of course, the suspect could have picked them up before he fled, but this is not likely in a crime of passion, especially in this case where the assailant abducted the second victim prior to fleeing the crime scene.

A handgun is an impersonal weapon to use when killing someone. You can stand at a reasonable distance, detached from the victim, and end that person's life without getting too dirty in the process, save for the gunpowder residue that is inevitably deposited on the hands of the attacker. But in this instance it was personal; very personal, indeed. The suspect knew the victims, and on this day, when he entered the victims' residence through the open garage door and knocked on the kitchen entry, he was met face to face by the first victim. The suspect immediately raised and discharged his revolver, the bullet striking the male victim in the face, causing him to fall backward onto the kitchen floor between the kitchen table and the window. Just for good measure and to make sure the job was finished, the suspect stood over the victim and pumped one more round into his right side. Then the suspect left the male victim there for dead and went looking for the object of his search.

Short on running money, the suspect, oddly enough, did take the time to raid the victims' coin jar, knocking it over and depositing pennies all over the floor of the house, or maybe he just knocked it over in the struggle. In any case, we know he was short on money because he and his accomplice, who picked him up from behind the store where he left the female victim, robbed several sandwich shops in the nearby metropolitan area during their flight to the hills.

We had put out the suspect's vehicle in a statewide bulletin, or "be on the lookout for" (BOLO), and a local police officer halfway across our state recognized it. Thanks to their great work, we took the suspect into custody without incident. When we were transporting the suspect back to our jurisdiction following his arrest, the gunman said, "If you take the needle off of the table, I'll tell you everything you want to know," meaning if we didn't seek the death penalty, he'd talk. Well, we came to find out that he was terminally ill and was going to die in custody before he ever exhausted his appeals, so we took him up on his offer.

He received two life sentences without the possibility of parole and ended up dying within the year.

Back in 1996, now twenty years ago, a popular book titled *Taking Back Our Streets: Fighting Crime in America* was written by former Philadelphia Police Commissioner turned LAPD Chief Willie L. Williams. The ideas presented in that book about community-oriented policing, neighbors helping neighbors, and getting involved in the solution to the problem still ring true today, and that is largely what the Street Crimes and Gang Enforcement division is about.

If you are a police officer long enough, have a demonstrated track record in earning the trust of the citizens you protect, and display a knack for combating the distribution of street-level drugs and curbing gang activity, you might be invited to become part of a Street Crimes and Gang Enforcement unit within your agency.

Street Crimes and Gang Enforcement officers usually wear plain clothes, carry their weapons concealed, and drive unmarked police vehicles with regular license plates. They're often referred to in pop culture as the "jump out boys" or "jump out team" because they roll up on the criminal activity, jump out, and confront the suspects or chase them on foot. The idea is to be less obvious, less visible, to members of street gangs and corner drug pushers in hopes of catching them with their pants down (in the act of committing crimes). But more than that, these officers are well known in the community among its law-abiding citizens, have earned their trust, and are often from diverse backgrounds and representative of the community they serve. As a result, law-abiding citizens are more apt to provide information to these officers than to the average uniformed police officer, whom they would not trust—information such that if it came back to the bad guys in the neighborhood, it could make life very difficult for the informant.

Toward the end of my career, I had the opportunity to belong to one of these units and work directly with members of specific neighborhoods in our city that had significant problems with street crime and drug dealing. So what is "street crime"? And what makes it different than any other crime committed against a person or property? "Street crime" is really just a catch-all term to identify and categorize any crime that happens in a public place. That's really all there is to it. It's very often combined with "gang enforcement" because street gangs are usually involved directly or indirectly with crimes that occur on the streets of a community.

In the area where I worked we had several street gangs, most of which were loosely affiliated with the larger gangs of the same name in a nearby metropolitan city. We also experienced a lot of spillover from the gangs in the metro area who traveled to our city to commit crimes where they were not known or, in their minds, they would meet with less response from law enforcement. These street gangs were usually comprised of members from a specific race or ethnicity, though rules regarding membership were often overlooked if the potential member brought something to their criminal activity that they valued. Additionally, there were gangs that, instead of affiliating with a specific ethnicity, rallied around a lifestyle or activity of some kind, like a recreational vehicle or music group; for example, biker gangs. In reality, no matter what the affiliation or makeup, they all had something in common: they used their illegal fraternity as a cover for or reason for committing crimes against the good people of the city.

One incident involving a street gang that took place in our community stands out in my mind. I was a detective at the time and on call to respond to any incidents requiring the involvement of the CID. On this night, I was called out to investigate and actively work the scene of an armed robbery that occurred in the parking lot of one of our big discount stores.

When I arrived on scene, I was briefed by responding officers and learned that a nurse, who had just completed her shift at our city's hospital, had been approached from behind in the parking lot of a "big box" store by two men wearing black and gold bandanas over their faces, one of whom was brandishing a handgun. When the nurse turned to see who was behind her, the barrel of the gun was placed on the tip of her nose and she was ordered to hand over her purse. The nurse freaked out, as would anyone in that situation, and threw her purse and cell phone at the suspects and ran screaming toward the store. Well, fortunately, this scared the suspects, who obviously weren't very experienced at this sort of thing, and they ran in the opposite direction of the store and were picked up by another gang member who was waiting and watching from their getaway vehicle nearby.

In their haste to leave, the suspects left one of their associates, who had gone inside the store to use the restroom, in the store. Once the heat died down from responding units, the suspects circled back around and picked the guy up, and then hightailed it back to the metro area via the interstate system. As luck would have it, the metropolitan gang task force stopped the suspects later that night, but didn't know that they had been involved in an armed robbery in our city. They did, however, fill out field identification cards on all of the occupants of the vehicle, and as a result there was a delayed hit once we entered our information into NCIC, a computerized index of criminal justice information.

So with the help of our colleagues in the metro area, we were able to locate the suspects in the armed robbery and take them into custody. In facilitating those arrests, we also gained some valuable intelligence on the gang the suspects belonged to, including their complete manifesto, apparel and jewelry used to demonstrate affiliation with the gang when worn, weapons, and other gang paraphernalia.

One of the gang members involved was an adult, while the other three were juveniles. On the day of the hearing in juvenile court, gang members filed into the courtroom wearing their colors in an obvious attempt to intimidate the victim (the nurse) who was scheduled to testify against their fellow gang members. I was monitoring the courtroom specifically to prevent this kind of intimidation from occurring, and I had a plan.

Most of the gang members who showed up were juveniles and it was a school day where they lived. Additionally, they had been transported to the hearing by an adult who knew the gang members were supposed to be in school. So I arrested all of them, the juveniles for truancy and the adult for contributing to the delinquency of minors. These charges were based in fact and much easier to prove than witness intimidation. That said, the result was the same. I was able to clear the gang element from the courtroom and by doing so ensure that the witness was not intimidated when she appeared and took the stand.

All of the suspects were convicted and the adult in the case went away for a long time. Of course, we seized his car and auctioned it off, and destroyed the weapons used in the commission of the crime. It was just another step in working to solve the gang and street crime problem in our community.

Many people know and understand what I mean when I say "narcotics," but few could define what is meant by the word "vice." In law enforcement parlance, the "vice" in "vice and narcotics" refers to crimes ranging from prostitution and untaxed liquor sold in "shot houses" to loan sharking, protection rackets, sports books, gambling, and more specifically the running of numbers games, crap games, punch boards, and even video poker machines that pay off in the back room of convenience stores, pool halls, and bars. Heck, it could even encompass a vending racket where machines are stocked with stolen product that is untaxed, overpriced, and forced on the establishments that house them. In the end, it's all about making easy money. That's why many of these schemes are favorites of organized crime.

Sound like fun? Then maybe one day you might want to join your agency's Vice and Narcotics unit, or Vice for short. Television has popularized these squads of misfit cops that appear dirty, disheveled, and inked up in shows like *The Shield* and *The Wire*. But like most jobs in law enforcement, the hours are long, the assignments can stretch out over months, you have to flip and manage informants (controlling the actions of criminals who are unpredictable and unreliable), the action usually comes in short bursts, and the paperwork, evidence collection, and court time is endless. So you will pay a personal price for your interest in this kind of enforcement.

I was exposed to our Vice and Narcotics unit early in my career during my field training rotation, spending a week with these guys. During my brief tenure with them, we conducted a prostitution sting where we made arrangements with a hotel to use two rooms that were joined, set up video and audio recording equipment, then called escort services and had them come to the room we had set up, complete with an informant. When the deed was starting to go down, no pun intended, we'd bust in and arrest the prostitute and her driver/pimp outside. Often we'd be able to charge them with other crimes from drug possession to weapons possession in addition to prostitution. We'd do this repeatedly until we reached the end of our shift, or just got tired of it.

I also spent time with them riding along on controlled purchases (drug buys), and I sat in on interviews where low-level dealers had been caught by patrol and were flipped and given the opportunity to work off their charges by arranging and participating in drug buys designed to build cases against dealers up the food chain. The idea is to make cases at all of these different levels until you finally reach the top, if possible. Of course, it goes without saying that this is dangerous work, and the farther you go, the more sophisticated and dangerous the game becomes. Suffice it to say that high-powered drug dealers, drug rings, and organized crime aficionados do not like their cash cow being screwed with while it's being milked.

Many informants, officers, detectives, dealers, mobsters, gangsters, and corrupt officials have lost their lives while involved in vice and narcotics investigations at the local, state, and federal level. And in addition to the obvious dangers, there is also the potential that you, the Vice officer or detective, will, under the intense pressure that comes with this type of work, lose sight of the line between the good guys and the bad guys, becoming a drug user or dealer yourself. Some guys, lured by the quick money, even end up working for the bad guys, covering up for them and taking payoffs to look the other way, or spending their time taking out the competition. All of these things really happen in the real world and are only slightly divorced from the fictional characters you've seen on television.

The work can be frustrating too. As soon as you put a few dealers away, there will be new players who have stepped up to take their place. And chances are they've learned a few lessons from the mistakes of their predecessors, and these new guys will be more sophisticated and harder to catch.

26

HATE GROUPS AND HATE CRIMES

For as long as poverty and ignorance have pervaded communities and the lives of people, hate groups and hate crimes have existed. In America, when we hear these terms used, we immediately think of fringe groups like the Ku Klux Klan, the Black Panthers, the Symbionese Liberation Army (SLA), the Irish Republican Army (IRA), the American Nazi Party (ANP), neo-Nazis, skinheads, the alt-right, nationalists, and many more. Historically, these are all good examples of hate groups and movements in the United States, but many of these groups are no longer active, are nonexistent, or have so few members that they do not pose the threat they once did, but that doesn't mean their seeds have ceased to find purchase in our soil or that new hate groups are not rising up to take their place. Take the new alt-right movement in the United States, for example. It's up to law enforcement and the various groups that aid police in this country to remain vigilant and monitor hate groups and hate crimes wherever they rear their ugly heads.

One such group that you should become familiar with and whose intelligence has served to educate countless law enforcement agencies and their officers is the Southern Poverty Law Center, founded by well-known civil rights attorney, activist, and combatant of hate Morris Dees. Thanks to organizations like the SPLC, these hate groups have a hard time flying under the radar and are more quickly exposed to the public and law enforcement officers than ever before.

Today we cops face fewer threats from hate groups like the KKK, ANP, and SLA. Instead, we are seeing a new breed of hate groups cropping up across this county with nationalistic agendas and rhetoric that is dangerous and often loosely disguised in discussions about the US Constitution and the right to gun ownership. You may have heard of some of these. They usually have words like "militia" in their names or fly confederate battle flags from their cars emblazoned with stickers like "Don't Tread on Me," taking slogans from previous conflicts out of context and attempting to hide prejudice and hate under the guise of "heritage." And if these new and volatile hate groups weren't scary enough, there are the members of the "sovereign citizens" movement who claim they owe no allegiance to any government, they don't have to pay taxes, they don't need a driver's license, they don't have to register their vehicles in the states where they live, and even go as far as to claim national landmarks and federally protected lands as their own—national parks, wildlife refuges, and national wonders that the government has set aside for all of us to enjoy for years to come with our families and friends.

If you haven't already concluded for yourself how these new hate groups pose a threat to law enforcement, let me shine some light on the subject for you. First, imagine attempting a traffic stop of an individual who doesn't recognize your authority as a police officer, and as such won't yield to your emergency equipment, or if he or she does, will attempt to engage you in a debate over the homemade driver's license issued by the fictitious state this individual has created, the same place his or her cardboard vehicle registration came from and whose laws only he or she knows.

If that is not problematic enough for you, then imagine this individual's anger growing when you attempt to enlighten him or her as to the actual law in your jurisdiction and state. Before you know it, this person is brandishing a gun, which, of course, he or she doesn't have a permit for, and threatening you with: "You're not going to take me in, I'm not subject to the laws of your republic or to your so-called authority," and you've now got a standoff that could double for a scene in an old wild west motion picture, complete with six shooters and chock-full of crazy bravado.

It's a dangerous scenario and one you might actually face as a police officer in the twenty-first century in America. If that was the only new hate group or radical-leaning contingent you had to face as a cop, that would be enough. But unfortunately, that is just the tip of the iceberg. Racial tension and nationalistic ideologies are at an all-time high in the

United States in this second decade of the new millennium. And regardless of your personal political leanings or views on immigration reform or the Black Lives Matter movement, or even the gun lobby and Second Amendment activists, as a police officer, you will have to protect the rights of all of these groups to hold and espouse their views, all the while knowing that in this dangerous climate, you, the police officer, are becoming the target of all of them.

Many of these groups use their self-proclaimed outrage and righteousness to justify bad behavior, unlawful protests, riots, looting, and violence aimed directly at you, the police officer, regardless of your race, ethnicity, or careful application of the laws you are sworn to uphold and enforce. Ideally, we, the populace, learn lessons from history and thereby avoid repeating it. However, we don't live in an ideal age and locale in America. So if you are going to be a police officer, know this.

Your application of force, justified or not, will be highly scrutinized, you will not be given the benefit of the doubt regarding your actions, and in a best-case scenario, you will be stripped of your badge, gun, and authority, and tried in the court of public opinion. In the worst case, you'll be arrested and charged criminally, and even if you are found innocent and reinstated, your life, reputation, perceived integrity, and those of your family will have already been destroyed. Ask yourself this question, "Am I really prepared to pay that price?" Good food for thought, huh?

27

USING FORCE

My First Wrestling Match

When you are a recruit or trainee you're told by your FTO that "it's not a question of if you will have a physical confrontation with a suspect on the street; it's only a question of when."

I was on patrol in a rough area of the city commonly referred to by officers and citizens alike as "Hard Bargain." This nook was about four square city blocks and had earned its name. The neighborhood's southern boundary was a state highway, while its northern boundary was a narrow two-lane road that paralleled a cemetery. Numbered avenues to the east and west bordered the area. Within the street grid were three little streets running east and west.

One street was a dead end and the other two were through streets. Most of the east and west streets were very narrow and only allowed enough room for one vehicle to pass if cars were parked on the shoulder, which was the case most nights.

The neighborhood earned its reputation in times past when after-hours clubs and shotgun houses (low-cost, narrow houses where you can see through from the front door to the back door) were predominant in the area. It was not unusual for full-scale riots to break out when police arrived in response to drunken confrontations over crap games, women, and common domestic disputes. Responding officers usually had to retreat and regroup amid a barrage of flying beer bottles, bricks, and rocks. In fact, my first patrol car, a 1995 Chevrolet Lumina, of which I was the sixth owner, had a large dent in the left front fender where a flying beer bottle had barely missed a cop just arriving on scene and exited his unit at one of the Hard Bargain joints.

The night of my first wrestling match with a suspect, I was on patrol in Hard Bargain. I was cruising the area very slowly, windows down, looking for criminal activity. I had my seatbelt off so I could jump out of my patrol car quickly in the event a suspect spotted me and ran. I turned down one of the narrow streets, and noticed the universal symbol letting all who care know that drugs were sold on this corner—a pair of tennis shoes draped over a low power line by their laces. I crept to a stop at the opposite end of the street to take a look back.

There, at a known drug house, I saw a male subject whom citizens in the neighborhood referred to as "Little Bubba." Little Bubba was wearing an overcoat that hung almost to his feet, with a cord leading from a Walkman cassette player to full-ear headphones over his ears. He was dancing around, kind of shuffling, in the middle of the avenue, causing passing cars to swerve into the oncoming lane of traffic or onto the sidewalk to avoid hitting him.

I radioed dispatch, advising my location and the nature of the call (Speak to Subject). I got out of my patrol unit and called to him saying, "Hey partner, come on over here and talk to me for a second." I motioned for him to come over to the sidewalk. Little Bubba came over kind of half shuffling and staggering. As soon as he was within two feet of me I was just about bowled over by the stench of alcohol. This did not particularly shock me as many of the men in this neighborhood were constantly drinking liquor.

I asked Little Bubba to remove his headphones, which he did, and told him that I didn't have an issue with his dancing, but I would like for him to do it on the sidewalk, rather than in traffic. Already, I could have taken Little Bubba into custody for public intoxication, as he was clearly unable to care for his own safety. However, in neighborhoods like Hard Bargain, it's sometimes best to let the little things go, because one day you might need to obtain valuable information from a subject regarding a serious offense. If you punk him out over public intoxication every time you see him on the street drunk, his response to you in your time of need will likely be, "I didn't see nothing, man."

So my game plan was not to take Little Bubba to jail but rather to get him out of the street and safely to a residence, front yard, or onto the sidewalk. As a matter of routine, I asked him for his identification so I could have him checked for active warrants. This is an officer safety issue, and, after all, I was in Hard Bargain alone at night. I also asked Little Bubba if he had been drinking, which in hindsight was a stupid question. I had already established the answer to that interrogatory when he initially walked up to me.

Little Bubba said that he had not been drinking and was not going to give me his identification or speak with me further. He then turned away from me and began walking down the narrow street. I closed the distance quickly between us and grabbed him by his left arm, now with the intent to take him into custody for public intoxication. His reaction was to jerk his arm away from me, which is a form of resistance.

At this point Little Bubba had become noncompliant. Criminals sense and look for weakness to exploit. To condone this behavior would have demonstrated weakness on my part. The perception of strength and control is always very important for officers, and even more essential when patroling an area like Hard Bargain.

Officers are trained at the police academy to respond to noncompliance on the part of citizens or suspects by accessing a Use of Force Continuum that they've had ingrained in them and memorized. Eventually, you respond to noncompliant actions using the continuum without even thinking about it. It becomes rote. This continuum varies from state to state and agency to agency, but this is generally how it goes.

The nonresistant action of compliance is met with officer presence. The officer appears in the presence of the complainant or suspect and presents with a professional bearing. The second action on the Use of Force Continuum is verbal resistance and is met by the officer with verbal commands, which should be clear and deliberate. Moving up the continuum, the next action is passive resistance, to which the officer applies soft-hand techniques, or Pressure Point Control Tactics (PPCT) that include come-along holds and wrist locks. You might also find chemical weapons on this level, like the commonly referred to tear gas or pepper spray. In professional terms, here we are referring to CS or chemicals like 2-chlorobenzalmalononitrile. CS causes the eyes to burn and tear up, and the mucous membranes to discharge, causing a lot of coughing and congestion, temporarily incapacitating a subject. Pepper spray comes in different forms and applications. In our department we used a single-stream application that consisted of the previously mentioned CS and another agent called oleo-capsicum (OC), which causes an extreme burning sensation.

The fourth action on the Use of Force Continuum is active resistance, which is met by officers with hard-hand techniques like strikes and takedowns, and may even include the use of less-than or less-lethal weapons. Examples of these types of weapons might include the retractable steel baton (ASP), the straight stick (baton), the PR-24 (a baton with a right-angle handle), the X-26 Advanced Taser (device that delivers a 50,000-volt electrical charge) designed to create muscle and pain compliance, and even a shotgun deploying a bean-bag round (a small projectile consisting of a cotton bag full of small pellets) that delivers an impact designed to temporarily incapacitate or stun a subject.

Finally, the last step and highest action on the Use of Force Continuum is a deadly force assault, which is met by the officer with lethal force, meaning firearms and strikes to lethal areas of the subject's body.

Ideally, you start at the bottom and move to the top as needed. At any time you can progress up the continuum and move back down the continuum depending on whether or not the citizen or suspect becomes more noncompliant or more compliant. In the state where I worked, we had the plus-one rule, where an officer could elect to move up one level or down one level on the continuum from the level of resistance in terms of his response. This gives the officer some flexibility when he or she encounters resistance that straddles the various levels of the continuum. I think you've got the idea now, so back to Little Bubba.

Again I took hold of his arm, which he promptly jerked away from me, and then he continued walking into the front yard of a residence. For the third time, I grabbed Little Bubba, this time placing him in an arm bar, and I attempted to take him to the ground to effect the arrest. Little Bubba had different plans. He reached in his overcoat with his free hand and pulled out a full beer bottle. His intent was clearly to hit me over the head with it.

It was on! My first wrestling match began. While I wrestled with Little Bubba, attempting to get him into an arm bar and on the ground in a facedown position, I managed to radio for a backup unit. However, I made the mistake of giving the location where I had stopped my patrol unit, rather than where Little Bubba and I had ended up wrestling around, in the front yard of a residence four houses west of my initial location.

Immediately following my request for backup, I heard the sirens start to wail. That was a welcome sound; I knew that help was close. I'm sure my request for additional units sounded urgent amid my struggle with Little Bubba. I certainly know it was regarded as urgent because I didn't follow up the request with the standard "nonemergency traffic" statement. When an officer calls for backup in an ordinary situation—for example, when he or she is going to take someone into custody who is cooperative—the officer requests a backup unit "nonemergency." When the request for backup is not followed by the phrase "nonemergency," it is assumed that units answering the officer's call should respond code 3, Emergency Traffic.

Meanwhile, I managed to get both of Little Bubba's arms locked to his side with the beer bottle still clutched in his right hand ready to bean me if the opportunity presented itself. My chest was against his back. Little Bubba was short but stout and surprisingly strong. I managed to keep his arms pinned to his side until one of my fellow officers found me, four houses away from my patrol car where this incident began.

I continued to grip Little Bubba's left arm while the other officer grasped his right arm. But Little Bubba was not about to give up so easily. He continued to struggle, and we all tumbled to the ground in a tangled knot of arms and legs in the middle of the narrow street.

Little Bubba's beer bottle went flying and smashed on the asphalt, glass shattering and beer scattering all over the place. Fortunately, we were able to avoid the glass when we took Little Bubba to the ground, and within a few seconds, I snapped the cuffs on him and took a gulp of air, which I sorely needed. Little Bubba was unhappy, but quit struggling after the cuffs went on. He wasn't saying much, believe it or not, because he was very drunk and probably dazed after all of the excitement.

Finally raising my head from my kneeling position over Little Bubba, who was facedown in the street, I saw the front bumper number of my shift lieutenant's patrol car. The lieutenant, "Lieu," as we called him, asked if I was okay. Thankfully, I was able to report that I was okay.

"Alright then, get him out of here," Lieu said urgently. An unwanted audience had begun to form. People were coming out of their houses in their bathrobes and nightclothes to see what was going on. We were about to be overwhelmed by the sheer number of people, some of whom could have been Little Bubba's friends or family. We didn't know and didn't want to find out this way. What we did know, however, from past history, was that it wouldn't take long for an impromptu riot to develop. Hard Bargain citizens didn't like the "PoPo," as they called us.

I'm sure my uniform was dirty from the melee, but I didn't have time to brush myself off. I quickly searched Little Bubba, asking him if he had any items in his pocket that could potentially poke or stick me, meaning hypodermic needles often used to inject illegal narcotics like methamphetamine or heroin, and put him in my patrol car. Not surprisingly, the search revealed numerous crack pipes, bottles of alcohol, and a large ball of hard, white powder in a plastic baggie. The large, white ball could have been crack cocaine or soap. I'd have to send it to the lab to be sure. Some small-time drug dealers would sell soap to naive people as crack, which was also a crime. Obviously, if you were sold soap for a large sum of money, you might get pissed off and come back to the dealer for an explanation, or worse. This was often the jump-off point for a violent encounter, which is exactly why the law was enacted.

Aside from the predictable items recovered when I searched him, there was also a rather strange assortment of trinkets, talismans, and oddities in Little Bubba's overcoat. Among these were mothballs (he often smoked these), bottles of his own urine, and a white substance I believed to be semen. Little Bubba was mentally unstable and obviously a very strange guy.

I had a bit of an adrenaline rush going following the incident, but there was no time to think about that. I just threw the car in gear and pointed it in the direction of the Criminal Justice Center. Upon arrival, I filled out the short booking sheet, put Little Bubba in a holding cell, and unwound with a cup of coffee. Following my much-needed break, I charged Little Bubba with assaulting a police officer, public intoxication, possession of drug paraphernalia, and resisting stop, frisk, halt.

I learned several things from my first hands-on confrontation. Number one, make sure you update communications when your location changes. Number two, when possible, anticipate the need for backup and request it before there is an urgent need for assistance. And finally, expect the unexpected, especially when dealing with subjects on the street in a high-crime area where foot traffic is predominant.

Little Bubba was one of our frequent flyers. A few months later he assaulted his own mother, barricaded himself in her house, and refused to come out. No one really knew why. Several officers responded to the scene, and after a thirty-minute standoff Little Bubba finally emerged, sporting a wooden broom handle and a Bible in each hand, like Moses before he parted the Red Sea. Again, his peculiar behavior got the best of him. Because his hands were occupied with his props, officers could quickly yank him off the front porch of the house, and put him facedown on the ground again—a position Little Bubba knows very well.

28

WHY DID YOU DO YOUR JOB? NOW I'LL HAVE TO WRITE YOU UP!

Why did you do your job? It may sound like a silly question; after all, aren't you supposed to do your duty as a police officer? The short answer is yes, but the command staff back at the police department want to have their cake and eat it too, meaning they want you to be effective without generating a complaint.

It's a difficult, almost impossible task to complete because the very nature of "doing your job" will often result in a complaint. Yes, the complaint may be unfounded, but there is a lot of public pressure on government officials (read "police administration" here) to answer the public's every complaint in the age of body cameras, digital audio recorders, cell phone videos, and the like. The pressure is even more extreme on elected officials (e.g., the city or county mayor and city manager) whose job depends on votes from constituents. Know that you will be the sacrificial lamb if you get frequent complaints, founded or unfounded, and try to avoid that becoming the case.

Chances are your department has policy that covers the informal, formal, and review processes resulting from complaints by the public about the department or specific officers. And like most policy, it's written in ambiguous fashion for the purpose of applying it any way the command staff wants to when convenient. In most disciplinary actions or internal investigations, you cannot count on a fair decision being rendered by the department, the city administration, the city's human resources department, or the public in general. If it's a situation that is going to end with someone's head being on the chopping block, trust me, it will be yours.

The best defense against the generation of complaints in law enforcement is to do the opposite of what you were hired to do, or at least strike a balance. Yes, you heard me correctly. That means doing the least amount possible with the least frequency. If you can do that, you might just survive.

Unfortunately, most of us get into this line of work for the right reasons. Our conscience and character requires that we do our job, which means someone is going to find fault with how or why we do what we do, and we are going to get complained about. Isn't being a police officer great!

It's usually about here that I make the statement that you should have sought a career in public service with the fire department instead of the police department. After all, everyone loves a firefighter. Everything they do is positive; they're always viewed as heroes. But the public, right or wrong, has a love/hate relationship with law enforcement. If they need you, they love you, but if you catch them breaking the law, they will respond to you with contempt and inevitably view you as the enemy. You know the old stereotype: all cops are corrupt, on the take, jerks, on and on it goes. If you're looking for a pat on the back in this job, get ready for a long wait.

Here's a good example. When responding to a call code 3 in a neighborhood, members of the homeowner's association will complain that you drove too fast, endangering the lives of joggers, children, and other such pedestrians. However, if you slow down and respond code 1, the individual/s who called you will complain that you didn't get to their residence fast enough. Get the point? You cannot win.

The informal complaint is the easiest to defend against if you have a supervisor who is worth their salt. Meaning, when people get their underpants in a knot over something you've done and call or request to speak with your supervisor, your supervisor will listen to them and then summarily tell them to "go fly a kite or whatever it is you do."

A stand-up supervisor will do this, but even such a supervisor will only be able to cover you for so long. Remember, he or she will have to answer for defending you if the incident reaches his or her supervisor. Your supervisor may respect and appreciate you for your loyalty and hard work, but eventually even he or she has to eat. On a side note, someone once said, "You can't eat honor and principle," and that person is right.

One thing is definitely true in all of these complaint situations. You have to be honest and demonstrate character. If you lie, even once, you're out. A police officer who can't be trusted to tell the truth and isn't known for his or her integrity is a castrated cop. Your career is as good as over. Tell the truth, even when it is going to hurt you. You'll have a much better chance of surviving the fallout.

Here's an example of this truth. There was an officer who ran into an object with her patrol unit and scraped up the side. It was an accident, and these are going to happen when you drive forty hours each week for a living. But instead of being honest about it, she claimed that she ran over a skateboard in the middle of the street that flew up in the air and scraped down the entire length of her patrol car. Not a really likely explanation. The story was investigated and when the truth came out, she was given a second chance to come clean, but she stuck to her story and lied her way to being fired. She was later the subject of a call for a subject with a gun, sitting on school property, drunk and off her medication, threatening suicide, presumably because her life fell apart after being fired from the department. Herein lies another important point. Do *not* let being a police officer define who you are or your entire life, because even if you stay in the department for the full ride and retire, you will not always be a police officer. One day you will once again be just an ordinary citizen like everyone else.

The formal complaint, or the written complaint, is the one your supervisor generally can't help you with at all. It will likely result in an internal investigation into your actions as a police officer, and even if you are exonerated in the end, you will likely be punished for the inconvenience you've put everyone through. The police administration needs to demonstrate to the complainant that they are doing something about the issue, meaning they have to give the complainant something, and that something is usually disciplinary action against you.

Maybe it will be a write-up, maybe a day or two off without pay. But trust me, you will pay. If you are wrapped up in these formal investigations too many times, you can expect to find your career swirling around in the toilet. Before you know it, you'll be living in the septic tank (bread line) looking for another job and hoping you qualify for unemployment.

Don't believe me? Well, just ask a retired officer who doesn't have a vested interest in fibbing and you'll find out. Don't even try to delude yourself into believing that the informal or formal complaint process will be fair, or that it matters that the complainant has a criminal history longer than your arm. The character and bad intentions of the complainant don't matter.

The officer is always, I repeat always, guilty until proven innocent when a complaint comes in, and it doesn't matter that everyone knows you are an officer of impeccable and demonstrated character, integrity, and honor. It won't matter that you possess a known record of figuratively shooting straight and being fair in all that you do in your personal and professional life. It just doesn't matter, and the sooner you accept that, the better off you'll be.

Here's another tip: don't bother with the grievance process or departmental hearing, unless you have an active association like the FOP or PBA, who have historically exercised power with your department in the area of arbitration, labor law, and so forth and done so successfully. If you will have to go it alone, just forget about it, it's a waste of time.

Chances are the leadership of your department has already made up their collective mind long before you enter the hearing. All you will really be doing by attending is pissing them off because they have to be there. Your retelling of the incident they've already read in the statement you were obliged to write, or your vocalized frustration, viewed as insubordination, won't advance your position. Again, it will only make them angry.

Take your lump, sign the disciplinary waiver, and go back to work. You'll be wiser for it and you'll try to avoid the situation in the future that resulted in your being there in the first place. Meaning, you'll try to slow down and avoid interacting with the public so much. Your proactive days in law enforcement are over, but don't lose any sleep over that fact. You're just maturing and growing as an officer. It's a growing pain. The system has just taught you a lesson the hard way. Unfortunately for the system, they've just lost another ally in the fight against crime. Congratulations, you've just taken one more step toward being the salty and jaded officer that many of us eventually become.

29

RACE, GENDER, AND THE ECONOMICS OF POLICING

"**H**ey officer, you're violating my civil rights because I'm a member of a minority," the suspect screams as you place them into the back of your patrol car in handcuffs. "This is just like Rodney King!" Here's another one of my favorites: "You wouldn't be taking me to jail if I was white!"

Yep, race, gender, and economics will all play a role in your daily job as a law enforcement officer. You will hear everything under the sun. If you're a black officer, you won't have to wait too long before you're called an "Uncle Tom" to your face by a member of your own ethnicity. If you're white and arrest a member of a minority, it will always be, in their eyes, because you are racially biased and never the result of their own bad choices and behavior.

It's bad enough that you'll have to endure that crap while dealing with the citizens in your community, but you'll also face it internally as well. You'll have to deal with backbiters, haters, old-school bigotry, and even gender bias in the police department. As a female officer, you'll often hear a male officer pipe up on the radio with, "Send me another unit dispatch, I have a female I need to search. Do we have a female officer on duty?" Never mind that female officers are expected to, and do, search males without the assistance of a male officer. Never mind that the male officers are taught how to properly search a female suspect to avoid being accused of misconduct.

Here's another favorite: "No dispatch, I don't need to be connected to the language line, just send Officer Lopez over here. He speaks Spanish, right?" Yep, officers will assume that because another officer has a Hispanic last name that he or she speaks Spanish fluently. In this day and age, it's just sad. In the department where I worked, we had an officer with a Hispanic last name, married to a woman of Hispanic ethnicity, who had four Hispanic children, who didn't speak a lick of Spanish. That is America.

And rest assured, it doesn't end with traditional prejudices; those are just the beginning. Socioeconomic bias will also factor in. For example, you'll often deal with individuals who live in government-subsidized housing, drive an expensive European import car, wear designer clothes, buy groceries with food stamps, smoke like a stack, drink like a fish, and sleep in because they don't have a job. What's wrong with that? Oh, and by the way, "Can I get my kids on the school lunch program?"

Here's a cop pop culture quiz for you. What's long, strong, and should remain unbroken? Okay, get your mind out of the gutter. I'm talking about the chain of command. In law enforcement, whether you are working for a local, state, or federal agency, you will be introduced and expected to follow a chain of command.

What is it? The chain of command is a military concept and for the record, law enforcement is a paramilitary organization. The chain of command is a hierarchical system of management. In policing, the officer is at the bottom. Proceeding up the chain within local and state law enforcement, with minor variations from agency to agency, you will find FTOs, corporals, sergeants, lieutenants, captains, majors, colonels, deputy chiefs, assistant chiefs, and the chief of police (the top cop in the agency). In some agencies, detectives (criminal investigators) are sergeants, and in others they are officers who work within the specialty of criminal investigations.

The officer receives direct supervision from someone one step above on the chain of command and indirect supervision from those individuals above the officer's immediate supervisor. Depending on where a law enforcement officer falls in the chain, he or she may supervise others (have subordinates) or may be an individual contributor specializing in an area and supporting the agency and its staff, but with no direct reports.

I would like to be able to tell you that how far up the chain of command you climb during your career in law enforcement will depend solely on your ambition, interests, how you test, your track record, and merit. However, the truth is that policing is still a male-dominated occupation and that the percentage of administrators broken down by gender is disproportionately heavy on the male side of the house.

Twenty-first-century law enforcement, like the rest of the public and private sector, is subject to laws related to labor, disabilities, gender and racial equality, and sexual harassment. That said, make no mistake, the "good old boy system" is still alive and well. Where female officers are concerned, you can usually break them down into two groups: female officers who can handle themselves and their responsibilities on the street as well as any male officer—read the label "bitch" and "lesbian" here— and then there's the female officers who are husband shopping. They are not considered capable by male officers, and are engaged 95 percent of the day in stroking the egos of their male counterparts. These women will be backed up on every call by male officers who will inevitably take over the call. These officers garner no respect and will only be as long for the job as it takes them to find a hook-up. Of the two, I would rather be assigned to the first group of female officers, thank you very much.

Even if you find yourself as a female officer among those recognized as proficient and professional, it's still difficult to break into physically demanding and dangerous specialties that are typically, and more importantly traditionally, assigned to male officers, such as Special Weapons and Tactics, Vice and Narcotics, Gang Enforcement, Street Crimes, Motorcycles, and so on. The men would rather see a female officer advance into units like Special Victims, Communications, Traffic, Records, Evidence, and Administration. You know, "jobs a woman can handle," and "men don't want."

30

RIDING THE STORM OF POSTTRAUMATIC STRESS DISORDER

In 2009, shortly after returning to the patrol division from a two-year stint as a detective assigned to the Major Crimes Unit, my uncle, who I was very close to, died unexpectedly in the Midwest. I had just taken him on a ride-along a few months earlier when he and my aunt were visiting from another state.

At first, I didn't realize his passing had hit me so hard, or had triggered something deep inside me that I had managed to suppress for so long. I immediately did what anyone who loses a close family member does: telephoned my immediate family members, made arrangements for leave from the police department to attend the funeral, called my cousins to express my sorrow for their loss and to let them know my family would be on the way to them as soon as we had packed and put gas in the car.

I met my sister and my parents in the town I grew up in so many years ago. We jumped into the car and I volunteered to drive for the first leg of the trip. We ran through the drive-thru of a local fast-food restaurant near the interstate and then hit the road. Since we were going to be travelling out of state, of course, I had my concealed carry (sidearm) and badge on my belt under my hoodie, in the unlikely event that we ran into trouble somewhere along the way. Certified law enforcement officers in the United States are allowed to carry a concealed weapon anywhere in the fifty states as a result of laws that facilitate interstate reciprocation. In hindsight, this was probably a time when I should have left the gun at home.

In the car heading north, it was not lost on me that this was the first time we, my immediate family, had been together in the same car on a road trip since my sister and I were kids. There are six years between my sister and me, and to say that we don't see eye to eye on current events, political or otherwise, would probably be an understatement. So there was already tension in the air. My father is equally opinionated and has become even more vocal in his later years, which scares all of us to death when he says something like "I think we should just carpet bomb the enemies of the US overseas." In reality, he has a good heart and would never hurt a fly, but he just doesn't understand that we are living in a different age where you cannot vocalize everything you think without experiencing possible repercussions, or at the very least, inconvenience. So, again, I was a little on edge to begin with on this journey.

I was still behind the wheel when about ninety miles into the trip I started perspiring and felt a dull pain in my arm accompanied by nausea. At first I just brushed it off as nothing and tried to ignore it. By the time we had crossed the state line and stopped at a visitor's center along the interstate, I was feeling really sick. I remember going to the restroom at the visitor's center and sitting in there, long after my mom, dad, and sister were already back in the car. I was dizzy as a duck and I thought I was going to vomit and then pass out on the floor. I willed myself to get up and head back to the car, not wanting to delay our departure. I told my family that I was feeling sick, maybe coming down with something, and that I thought my sister should drive. I put my earbuds in my ears, started up my MP3 player, cranked up the volume, closed my eyes, and crammed my head into a pillow against the passenger side window in the back seat, hoping that what I was experiencing would pass. I stayed in that position until we arrived at the hotel out of state.

If I had known then what I know now, I would have realized that I wasn't coming down with the flu, that I wasn't having a heart attack, but rather that I was having a panic attack related to the onset of PTSD. But at that point, I didn't have a clue, and I would have laughed at you if you had suggested that diagnosis to me.

Somehow, I made it through the funeral and managed to drive the family back home. I don't know how I succeeded in doing that, because every time we would cross a large bridge span over major river tributaries, I felt like the steel structure was closing in on me and that I was going to pass out, literally.

My department only allows an officer one day of leave when someone in their extended family dies, and three days if the person was a member of your immediate family. So I had to go right back to work the day we arrived home from the funeral.

I'll never forget that first morning back on the job. I was assigned to day shift when I left CID, as I had enough seniority to avoid working nights after seven years on the force. Day shift starts with roll call at 6 a.m. and in the winter, which it was, it's pitch-black outside when you arrive in the police department parking lot.

At my agency we were assigned take-home cars, meaning we didn't "hot seat," or share police units with other officers. I had my own assigned unit. However, I didn't live in the city where I worked, because frankly I couldn't afford to on a police officer's salary. So I lived in an adjoining county, which meant I had to leave my patrol car in the county of my agency and then take my personal vehicle (POV) home from there. I parked my car at a local truck stop on the county line to save gas in my POV by cutting down the mileage from my house to the truck stop.

The morning after returning from my uncle's funeral was cold, dark, and miserable, with bad road conditions due to freezing rain and sleet. It was not going to be a great day at work. I already had visions of multiple car crashes and traffic delays dancing in my head like rotten sugar plums. At approximately 4:45 a.m. I loaded my gear into the truck and set out for my patrol unit at the truck stop. I remember feeling dizzy again, like I had been while driving to the funeral the previous weekend, only this time driving conditions were hazardous and my sister wasn't there to take over for me. I struggled to stay in my lane and kept telling myself, "This is ridiculous, you've got this, Alley. You are okay! This is all in your head." By the time I reached the truck stop and transferred my gear to my patrol car, I was seriously thinking about calling in sick and going home, which is what I should have done.

But cops are invincible, right? We don't get sick, we muscle through any difficulty, and we adapt and overcome all challenges. And we certainly don't have panic attacks! Only nut jobs and weaklings are subject to those. As I have articulated before and I will say it again here, I was such an idiot! I was most certainly having a panic attack, and I had no business getting behind the wheel of that patrol car or trying to work in that condition. I needed to figure out what was wrong with me. I needed help, I just didn't know it yet. I was headed downhill, and fast.

By the time I made it to the police department and into the roll call room, I was literally resting my forehead on the roll call table. I was in bad shape. I was not "okay." Finally, I made a good decision. I told my shift sergeant that I was still not over the death of my uncle and the funeral that weekend and that I needed to take a sick day to rest and shake it all off. He checked to make sure we had enough officers to cover shift and then told me I could take off. On the way back to the truck stop in my patrol unit, I almost passed out twice and nearly ran off the road on both occasions. I made it to my POV, but had no sooner gotten onto the interstate that I started experiencing symptoms again, only this time, I decided I must be having a heart attack due to all the fatty, high-in-cholesterol fast food I had eaten over the years on patrol. I had just clogged my arteries, right? It was pouring freezing rain on the highway and still black outside. I pulled my truck to the shoulder, activated my hazard lights, got out and went around the passenger side and knelt down on my knees in the saturated ground and mud that was the ditch. The water was pouring over my head, I was vomiting, and I was still in uniform. Did anyone stop to see if the cop on her knees on the side of the road in the rain storm was okay? Nope. "It figures," was what I thought at the time. They were probably secretly laughing and enjoying my misery. I called my life partner, Jacki, on my cell phone, and she managed to talk me back to our town, where I stopped at the ER and was checked out to make sure I wasn't in cardiac arrest, which, as we know of course, I wasn't.

The next day, I went to my general practitioner who told me that I was likely having a panic attack and that she would prescribe me an antidepressant and a medication for nausea. She also advised that I speak with a counselor or psychologist. I received a note from her to justify my time off from work, got my prescription filled at the local pharmacy, and headed home. I also have to say that Jacki was with me all the way, as she had always been during my law enforcement career, driving me to my appointment and making sure I was taking my meds and resting. There was just one problem. My general practitioner was not a psychiatrist and, of course, which antidepressant will work for you is highly individualized. We got it wrong the first time and the next four days were a roller-coaster ride.

I went four days without sleep and I started having crazy thoughts. By the fourth night on this new medication and without any sleep I was literally fighting off thoughts of grabbing a kitchen knife and stabbing Jacki. I was experiencing a terrible acid burn in all my appendages, which I would later learn was a result of sleep deprivation and a massive dump of cortisol and adrenaline in my system. I'm not a doctor, but I can tell you from personal experience, research, and consulting with medical professionals that the body dumps cortisol and adrenaline into a person's body when that person is confronted with a life-threatening altercation, and police officers experience this dump over and over again, day after day, for years on end. The result is that your internal accelerator gets stuck in the down position, resulting in PTSD and a constant feeling that you have to run or defend yourself even when you are not being threatened. This is called the "fight-or-flight" response and is a recognized symptom of PTSD among medical professionals who treat soldiers and first-responders—like, uh, police officers, let's say.

I clicked on the light resting on the night table by our bed, went to the living room and woke Jacki up, told her I needed to go to the hospital and I needed to go now. She had been sleeping on the sofa in our family room because she was afraid of me in this unhinged state. I had already locked up my firearms and gave her the key, because I knew something was seriously wrong and I didn't trust myself.

We climbed in the car—it was two in the morning—and drove to the local ER, only this time I told the triage nurse that I was a police officer and that I was having a panic attack that I thought was related to my time on the force and suppression of a lot of emotions I had not let myself feel in working homicides, suicides, and other death investigations as a detective over the years, not to mention a critical incident that almost led to me having to take someone's life in the line of duty. I just hadn't dealt with any of it and my uncle's death had tipped the kettle over and now everything was running out all at once.

Boy, was I lucky. The triage nurse I met that night in the ER was a Navy veteran and corpsman who had been forward deployed to Iraq and Afghanistan. He had treated numerous soldiers suffering from PTSD and he immediately and correctly diagnosed my problem based on the symptoms I was describing. He got me straight into a treatment room, by myself (he knew the importance of not putting me with other patients), and started an IV. Then he hit me with a good dose of Ativan, a CNS sedative that is used to treat anxiety, insomnia as a result of anxiety, and nausea. How perfect was that! It only takes five minutes for that drug to take effect when administered intravenously and I have to tell you, I felt like someone had just draped a cold sheet over my entire body. For the first time in days, the choppy waves I had been riding receded and all around me emerged the serenity of a calm, glassy lake surrounded by snow-capped mountains.

That was only the first step though. Now that I had been treated and conditionally diagnosed, I needed to get to the psychiatric hospital in the nearby major metropolitan city and be assigned a bed and a real shrink (psychiatrist). I got in touch with my father and he agreed to drive me, as Jacki needed a break after four days of dealing with me on the edge.

Dad drove me to the hospital, I went through a short screening process for self-committal, and then I headed up to the ward. Because of my education and career, I was assigned to the highest functioning unit and given, once again, my own room. That said, I still had to suffer the humiliation that goes along with being an inpatient in a mental hospital. Fortunately, I was only there for a day and a half. I was paired with a great doctor, who I credit with saving my life, prescribed sleep aids and the right antidepressant for my condition, and then allowed to go home just as soon as I stabilized. I have to tell you, I was scared to leave; I wasn't sure I was going to be okay after just a day and a half, but my doc knew what she was doing, and in spite of my fears, I willed myself, as in the past, to put one foot in front of the other and walk out the hospital door.

At first, after I returned home, I couldn't drive. Every time I got behind the wheel I started having a panic attack and everything made me nervous: simple sounds you hear when driving, passing traffic, emergency vehicles, backfiring mufflers. I felt like the inside of the car was closing in on me. Slowly but surely, I started making short drives with my spouse in the passenger seat encouraging me. If learning how to drive comfortably again wasn't enough, I also had to overcome a bout of agoraphobia, where you are afraid to leave the house. Even a trip to a local box store where I had to be around a lot of people was hard. I remember having to jam my hands in the front pockets of my jeans to make sure I didn't act on the urge to punch someone for no reason. Again, the old fight-or-flight mechanism resulting from too much cortisol and adrenaline being generated in my body when I was in panic mode. Little by little though, as the medicine I was taking began to take effect, those feelings subsided and gave way to feeling normal again.

Six weeks later, after a bumpy but effective recovery, I was back on duty and working the street. How, you ask, was that possible after all I had been through? Wasn't the police department concerned about my ability to function on the job and exercise good judgment without going off the deep end? Those are good questions, and I'll answer them in the next chapter, but suffice it to say the medication made all the difference and restored my mental health and well-being. My mental health professional assured me that I would be fine under pressure and on the job. She said that if I was going to have a problem it would be at home after work when I started to decompress, and not in the field. She was right.

31

SHOW NO WEAKNESS

Anyone who has ever raised or cared for chickens knows that when a bird is injured and bleeding, the other birds in the flock will attack it without mercy, and they will literally peck it to death. So remember, as a police officer among the many cops employed by your agency, you are just like that chicken. If you demonstrate weakness, appear to be injured, stumble and fall, make too many mistakes on the job, or become difficult to work with for any reason, you will be singled out and placed under a microscope and a tremendous amount of pressure until you are eventually driven from the officer ranks and out of the department.

You will crack and resign, or they will pursue you until the paper trail appears to be long enough to justify your termination. Either way, you are damaged goods, and they (the command staff) don't want you around anymore. You are a threat to the fiction, the myth, the perception of the tall-in-the-saddle and larger-than-life cowboy in the white hat that rides in to save the day, the hero that they (the leaders of the law enforcement profession) have created and perpetuated. It doesn't matter that it's erroneous or that no human being working under the heavy weight of the badge can endure a twenty-five-year career of pushing emotions down to the deepest regions of his or her psyche, his or her soul, without being affected by it. You are expected, required, to suffer alone and in silence, and when that doesn't work, to self-medicate with prescription drugs, alcohol, sex, gambling, or any other legal vice. It's okay, as long as you keep showing up and keep your mouth shut.

Sure, your agency will annually, during in-service (the minimum mandatory week of refresher training every department is required to hold to recertify their officers), remind you that if you are having psychological trouble you can take advantage of the Employee Assistance Program (EAP), but consider this. EAP is funded by the city and provides counselors for officers that need to discuss, via telephone, any emotional problems they are having. Of course, it's touted as being anonymous, but do the math. The counselors and their firm are under contract with your agency, your employer, and if you think they aren't reporting back to the department and taking part in what they would call an "Early Warning System" then you really do need psychological help.

In fact, if you believe that, I'd have to ask how you got hired on in the first place. All sarcasm aside, take my word for it, you would be just as well-served by saving your dime for the call to EAP and just walking into the chief of police's office and announcing that you were upset, sad, or emotionally distraught following a difficult call for service you responded to.

I followed the department and city's procedure when I returned to work following my hospital stay and recovery period and provided them with a letter from my board certified psychiatrist stating that I had been diagnosed with PTSD, was taking my prescribed medication, and was fit for duty. But surprise, surprise. A few weeks after my return to patrol, I was called into a meeting with the chief of police, the city's HR director, and other police supervisors, and told I would be placed on administrative leave pending the outcome of a Fitness for Duty Examination by a psychologist (not psychiatrist) of their choosing. You're following this, right? They are paying for it and will be receiving the results from a psychologist who is second-guessing a board certified psychiatrist. Sound a little suspect? Yep, it did to me too. And being a seasoned investigator and having been a detective in major crimes, I smelled this setup coming.

Later the city would even go so far as to contend that they never even knew I had a PTSD diagnosis. Unbelievable, you say? Well, some organizations and some people can lie and never be called to task for saying something they know is completely false and can be fact-checked. Don't believe it? Then you are not watching the nightly news, my friend.

So I did what any good investigator would do. I digitally recorded my consultation with the city's hired gun (psychologist), which is perfectly legal, because in our state only one party (that being me) is required to know the conversation is being recorded. But to keep things above board, I didn't keep it a secret from the psychologist; I told her what I was doing. She said she "would prefer it if I didn't record the evaluation," to which I responded, "duly noted," and continued to record.

Well, what do you know, a few weeks later when the city received their feedback from the psychologist, she concurred with the board certified psychiatrist that I was "Fit for Duty." Needless to say, the command staff was mad, but they had to reinstate me. It would be foolish though for you to think that that was the end of it, because it wasn't. I was just buying myself time, and I knew it. For the next two years, the department worked overtime to create a false "pattern" of behavior that would justify my termination. That's right. They chose to pursue disciplinary action over accommodating an officer who had been diagnosed with PTSD. Never mind the Americans with Disabilities Act (ADA) or my record of exemplary service and a multitude of commendations.

Here's another little tenet that every veteran police officer would likely agree with: "Show me a police officer who never receives a complaint and I'll show you a police officer who is not working." Get that? A police officer who is *not* doing his or her job. By its very nature, policing generates complaints. There will always be citizens (taxpayers) who are not satisfied with what their police department/agency and its officers do or don't do. It's generally a lose/lose occupation, not at all like being a firefighter, where everyone is always glad to see you.

When it comes to seeking out people holding the moral high ground in our country, I would not recommend looking toward the hill that city hall resides on, or even the police department administration, for that matter. Yes, there are good administrators and morally sound leaders in law enforcement, but there are some people who don't belong there as well and are lacking in the area of good intentions.

I can tell you that I have personally witnessed the railroading of several good officers simply because their personal health, largely as a result of being law enforcement officers, began to fail and the city was self-insured. Rather than take care of and support these officers, the city attempted to piece together false patterns of misbehavior and then terminate these officers. One was on a transplant waiting list, and the other was so sick he almost died. The first officer on the transplant list was fired on trumped-up charges, but after fighting the city for two long years and receiving his transplant, the city was forced by the courts to reinstate him, and he is still an officer to this day. Now, you can bet he'll never receive a promotion, but he will certainly not be fired again. As for the second officer, he fought the city at the same time he was on the verge of dying and won, managing to stay on at the department and recover from his surgery to the extent possible. He was never able to go back on patrol, but he is still a firearms instructor and a sergeant.

No officer in good standing should ever have to undergo what those officers went through. Those officers had to fight for their job and fight for their life at the same time. It was a travesty and a direct result of city and police department leadership that was entirely devoid of the character and morals they purported to uphold while thumping their chest and espousing self-righteous mottos.

So if the department wants to address every complaint you receive rather than disregard those complaints as unfounded, their typical unofficial and preferred response for officers who are in their good graces, they will. And not only will they address them, they will formally conduct their own internal investigation on every one with an internal review board where you are not entitled to have an attorney to represent you in the hearing. And what determination do you think they will come to if they want to show you to the door? You have violated departmental policy, and now they will have to terminate you. You are now the "bleeding chicken," my friend!

What is the moral of this chapter, you ask? "Don't be the bleeding chicken if you want to continue your career in law enforcement," but understand, you may be trading your own well-being, physical and mental health, for that shiny piece of tin you are so proud of on your chest.

POLICING IN TWENTY-FIRST-CENTURY AMERICA

I left policing at the start to the second decade of the twenty-first century in America, and in the years since, the profession of law enforcement has changed dramatically, and not necessarily for the better. These changes have been precipitated in large part due to incidents involving the use of deadly force by police against citizens and suspects in cities like Baltimore, Baton Rouge, Dallas, Milwaukee, Falcon Heights, a suburb of St. Paul, Minnesota, Tulsa, Charlotte-Mecklenburg, and others too numerous to mention. Some of these events have touched off discussions and protests involving issues of race, religion, and immigration. Many of these evolutions in policing have been influenced by public perception and stories appearing in the media and are not necessarily aligned with the realities experienced by law enforcement officers every day in the streets of the United States.

Frankly, when I entered policing at the outset of the new millennium, the pendulum regarding what was an acceptable use of force by law enforcement and in what situations had already begun to dramatically swing from the far, conservative right of the 1970s and 1980s to the extreme left of the 1990s and on. There have been numerous roll call table debates between officers as to whether or not these changes have been for the better. Many of those who are on the job believe that by tying the hands of the police to respond to crime with heavy restrictions, we (those of us living and working in America) are encouraging criminals to act and increase their presence without fear of repercussion from law enforcement and the courts. Others believe that these new, more restrictive policies and procedures protect the public from heavy-handed, Stormtrooper-like police forces that in their minds are ready to prey upon anyone who is not of a certain ethnicity or from a specific socioeconomic background. In their opinion, if officers will just "behave in a professional manner," these perceived excesses could be avoided.

The fact is, in my humble opinion and that of many leaders among the ranks of law enforcement, the majority of officers have always behaved in a professional and nonbiased manner in this country. There have been, admittedly, individual bad apples who have slipped through the cracks, and there have been forces in certain geographic regions in certain isolated decades that committed egregious, unlawful acts predicated on and directed against members of certain races and religions.

That said, no longer can officers in the United States believe that if they follow policy, procedure, and the law when they apply justified force to effect the arrest of a violent felon, they will be granted immunity from criminal prosecution, given the benefit of the doubt until an investigation proves otherwise, or not suffer the shame and humiliation of being figuratively and literally defrocked (having their badge and duty weapon taken away) and tried in the court of public opinion. As a result, law enforcement officers are faced with making a decision between intervening in an incident and risking their own and their families' well-being, and fulfilling their oath of office to protect the public and their property from harm. What would you do? From my perspective, I don't think I'd be signing up to become an officer these days and I'm extremely grateful that I'm standing on the outside looking in given the current climate. It's pretty hostile out there for cops.

Another troubling outcome related to these events, shown almost in real-time on television and the Internet, is that they provide an excuse for criminals to behave badly and in ways they wouldn't ordinarily, when they know that law enforcement resources in their community are strained and cannot respond to their crimes. This environment gives way to looting, vandalism, and other crimes against police, citizens, and property that are "off the chain." For example, under any other circumstances would a citizen believe that it's okay to overturn a police car and set it on fire, or break windows in a drugstore and steal everything inside the establishment? Or for that matter, directly attack a police officer with a hatchet or assault rifle? I don't think so.

The last time I reviewed the words of Representative John Lewis, Dr. Martin Luther King, and other prominent members of the Civil Rights Movement in the United States, peaceful protests, sit-ins, and marches weren't to be conducted in concert with rioting, bottle throwing, willful destruction of property, violence, and the unlawful blocking of public services and roadways. When Congressman Lewis crossed that bridge in Selma, he turned the other cheek when police beat him mercilessly and without cause. Those state troopers who participated in the action were amoral, and should have been fired and criminally charged for their behavior. But look at Rep. Lewis's example. He knew that violence and disorder only result in more violence and disorder.

So am I concerned about the safety of good, well-intended, professional law enforcement officers in America? Yes, I am. But I am also concerned for our level-headed, reasonable citizens from all ethnicities, religions, and backgrounds. Because their safety is also being compromised by knee-jerk reactions on both sides of the fence to perceived and real abuses and excesses of every kind—those perpetrated by police and those perpetrated by a criminal element.

I certainly don't pretend to have all the answers to resolve these issues, but I do believe that law enforcement administrators and community leaders and organizers who are willing to sit down with level heads and hearts to try to talk about these problems and work together toward their resolution are on the right track. We can't ignore the problems or their impact and put our heads in the sand, nor can we afford to react when emotions are high and refuse to apply logic and reason toward the resolution of these difficult issues. I really believe that together, with open hearts, open ears, open eyes, and open minds, we can solve any crisis between police and the communities they protect.

Let's hope that the leaders on both sides of the aisle on these issues feel the same way.

NOTE

1. MYTH VERSUS FACT

1. Rich Dittmar, "Syndrome Fighter Editorial," BPA Syndrome (Fighter, 1986).

INDEX

ABOUT THE AUTHOR

Alley **Evola** is a retired nine-year veteran of a mid-size police department in the southeast, serving a community with a population of nearly 100,000. She has served as a patrol officer, crime scene technician, field training officer, Flex unit (street-level gang/narcotics unit) officer, and detective assigned to the major crimes unit. She is an ACA-certified correctional manager, and has also worked in the area of partnership corrections for several years.

She is a graduate of TLETA (Tennessee Law Enforcement Training Academy) and maintains her POST (Peace Officer's Standards and Training Commission) certification in the state where she served. She is also a graduate of the Medicolegal Death Investigators Course at the University of St. Louis School of Medicine, a graduate of the first-line supervisor's course at the University of Tennessee, and a graduate of the Regional Counterdrug Training Academy in Meridian, Mississippi.

Evola is also a graduate of Middle Tennessee State University with a Bachelor of Science degree in mass communications with minors in English and speech. She has been employed as a staff writer for *The Tennessean*, the *Nashville Business Journal*, and the *Marshall County Tribune*.

She is the author of "A Simple Warrant Service," which appears with a collection of short stories in *American Blue*, compiled and edited by nationally renowned law enforcement trainer and author Ed Nowicki. She is also the author of *Ravenous, All-Knowing Bitch*, a collection of free-verse poetry.